Everyday Mathematics®

Study Links

Everyday Mathematics ®

Study Links

**The University of Chicago
School Mathematics Project**

SRA

A Division of *The McGraw-Hill Companies*

*Columbus, Ohio
Chicago, Illinois*

UCSMP Elementary Materials Component

Max Bell, Director

Authors

Max Bell
John Bretzlauf
Amy Dillard
Robert Hartfield
Andy Isaacs
James McBride, Director

Kathleen Pitvorec
Peter Saecker
Robert Balfanz*
William Carroll*
Sheila Sconiers*

Technical Art

Diana Barrie

First Edition only

Photo Credits

Phil Martin/Photography; National Aeronautics and Space Administration, p. 91
Cover: Bill Burningham/Photography; Photo Collage: Herman Adler Design Group

This material is based upon work supported by the National Science Foundation under Grant No. ESI-9252984. Any opinions, findings, and conclusions or recommendations expressed in this material are those of the authors and do not necessarily reflect the views of the National Science Foundation.

www.sra4kids.com

SRA/McGraw-Hill

A Division of The McGraw-Hill Companies

Send all inquiries to:
SRA/McGraw-Hill
P.O. Box 812960
Chicago, IL 60681

Printed in the United States of America.

ISBN 1-57039-972-7

2 3 4 5 6 7 8 9 VL 06 05 04 03 02 01

Contents

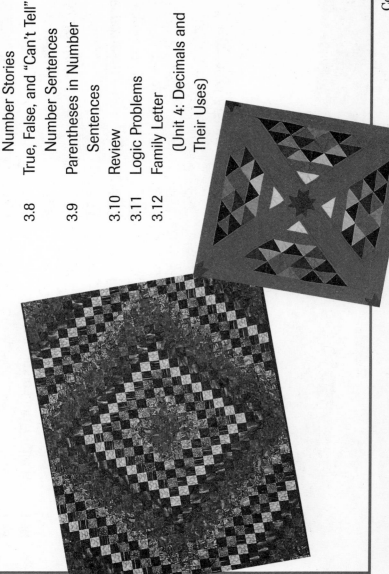

Family Letter

Introduction to Fourth Grade Everyday Mathematics®

Welcome to *Fourth Grade Everyday Mathematics*. It is part of an elementary school mathematics curriculum developed by the University of Chicago School Mathematics Project (UCSMP).

Everyday Mathematics offers students a broad background in mathematics. Some approaches in this program may differ from those you used as a student. However, the approaches the authors use are based on research results, field-test experiences, and the mathematics that students will need in the twenty-first century. Following are some program highlights:

▷ A problem-solving approach that uses mathematics in everyday situations

▷ A balance of independent activities that develop confidence and self-reliance, and partner and small-group activities that promote cooperative learning

▷ Concepts and skills introduced and reviewed throughout the school year, promoting retention through a variety of exposures

▷ Concepts and skills developed through hands-on activities

▷ Opportunities to discuss and communicate mathematically

▷ Frequent practice using games as an alternative to tedious drills

▷ Opportunities for home and school communication

Fourth Grade Everyday Mathematics emphasizes the following content:

Algebra and Uses of Variables Reading, writing, and solving number sentences

Algorithms and Procedures Exploring addition, subtraction, multiplication, and division methods; inventing individual procedures and algorithms; and experimenting with calculator procedures

Coordinate Systems and Other Reference Frames Using numbers in reference frames: number lines, coordinates, times, dates, latitude and longitude, and elevation above and below sea level

Exploring Data Collecting, organizing, displaying, and interpreting numerical data

Functions, Patterns, and Sequences Designing, exploring, and using geometric and number patterns

Use with Lesson 1.1.

Math Experiences Your Child Will Have This Year

The mathematics program we are using this year—*Everyday Mathematics*—will help your child appreciate how mathematics affects our daily lives and will prepare your child for making sound decisions in areas that involve mathematics. Experiences your child will have include the following:

▽ Collecting, displaying, and interpreting numerical information—for example, about the climate in the United States and other parts of the world; about the way people in other countries live; about mammals; and about the students in the class themselves

▽ Exploring the role of mathematics in geography—for example, using latitude and longitude to locate places in the world; using a map scale to find distances; and using a time-zone map to compare the time of day in various locations

▽ Developing methods for estimating the lengths, heights, and weights of objects; and practicing making accurate measurements

▽ Examining several methods for adding, subtracting, multiplying, and dividing numbers; and becoming proficient at using one of these methods for each operation

▽ Beginning the study of algebra and continuing the study of geometry

▽ Predicting the outcomes of events that occur by chance and checking the predictions by performing experiments

Throughout the year, you will receive Family Letters informing you of the mathematical content to be studied in each unit. Letters may include definitions of new terms as well as suggestions for at-home activities designed to reinforce skills. We are looking forward to an exciting year filled with discovery. You will enjoy seeing your child's mathematical understanding grow.

Geometry and Spatial Sense Developing an intuitive sense about 2- and 3-dimensional objects, their properties, uses, and relationships

Measures and Measurement Exploring and using metric and U.S. customary measures: linear, area, volume, weight; and exploring geographical measures

Numbers, Numeration, and Order Relations Reading, writing, and using whole numbers, fractions, decimals, percents, and negative numbers; and exploring scientific notation

Operations, Number Facts, and Number Systems Practicing addition and subtraction to proficiency; and developing multiplication and division skills

Problem Solving and Mathematical Modeling Investigating methods for solving problems using mathematics in everyday situations, such as travel, shopping, health, and sports

Unit 1: Naming and Constructing Geometric Figures

During the next two to three weeks, the class will study the geometry of 2-dimensional shapes. Students will examine definitions and properties of various shapes and the relationships between and among these shapes. Students will use compasses to construct shapes and to create their own geometric designs. In the process, they will develop an appreciation for geometric patterns and their many uses.

Please keep this Family Letter for reference as your child works through Unit 1.

Vocabulary

Important terms in Unit 1:

concave (nonconvex) polygon A polygon in which at least one vertex is "pushed in."

concave polygon

convex polygon A polygon in which all vertices are "pushed outward."

convex polygon

endpoint A point at the end of a line segment or a ray. A line segment is normally named using the letter labels of its end points.

line segment A straight path joining two points. The two points are called the endpoints of the segment.

parallelogram A quadrilateral that has two pairs of parallel sides. Opposite sides of a parallelogram are congruent.

polygon A closed, 2-dimensional figure that is made up of line segments joined end to end. The line segments of a polygon may not cross.

quadrangle or quadrilateral A polygon that has four sides and four angles.

ray A straight path that extends infinitely from a point called its endpoint.

rhombus A quadrilateral whose sides are all the same length.

trapezoid A quadrilateral that has exactly one pair of parallel sides.

vertex The point where the rays of an angle, the sides of a polygon, or the edges of a polyhedron meet.

Do-Anytime Activities

1. Help your child discover everyday uses of geometry as found in art, architecture, jewelry, toys, and so on.

2. See how many words your child can think of that have Greek/Latin prefixes such as *tri-, quad-, penta-, hexa-, octa-,* and so on.

3. Help your child think of different ways to draw or make figures without the use of a compass, protractor, or straightedge. For example, you can trace the bottom of a can to make a circle, bend a straw to form a triangle, or make different shapes with toothpicks.

4. Challenge your child to draw or build something, such as a toothpick bridge, using triangle and square shapes. Or show pictures of bridges and point out the triangle shapes used in bridges to provide support.

As You Help Your Child with Homework

As your child brings assignments home, you may want to go over the instructions together, clarifying them as necessary. The answers listed below will guide you through this unit's Study Links.

Study Link 1.2

1. Answers vary.
2. Answers vary.

Study Link 1.3

1. a. 12   b. 8
2. a. 6   b. 12   c. 4

Study Link 1.4

1. Sample answer:

2. a. yes   b. yes   c. yes   d. no
3. Sample answer:

4. Sample answer:

Study Link 1.5

a. D and O
b. All capital letters except D and O
c. Answers vary.
d. Answers vary.

Study Link 1.6

f   octagon
e   rhombus
h   right angle
c   trapezoid
a   square
i   equilateral triangle
d   parallel lines
g   pentagon
b   quadrangle

Study Link 1.7

1. Answers vary.
2. Answers vary.

Study Link 1.8

1. rhombus
2. rectangle
3. equilateral triangle
4. Answers vary.

Geometry in Your Home

Study Link
1.2

SRB
76 94

1. List at least 5 things in your home that remind you of line segments.

_____

_____

_____

_____

_____

2. Look for geometric patterns in your home. Sketch at least two of the patterns that you find. Write a description of the pattern for each of your drawings.

Shape Search

SRB
84–86

1. Study the figure at the right.

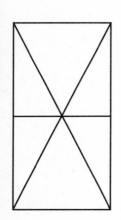

   a. How many triangles do you see?

   _____

   b. How many triangles have
   a right angle?

   _____

2. Study the figure at the right.

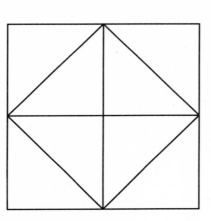

   a. How many squares do you see?

   _____

   b. How many triangles?

   _____

   c. How many rectangles
   that are not squares?

   _____

3. Make a 4 by 4 array of dots on the back of this page, like this but bigger:

   Make up a geometry puzzle like the one in Problem 2. Draw line segments
   to connect some of the dots in your array. Then ask someone to count the
   number of triangles in your puzzle.

Use with Lesson 1.3.

7

Classifying Quadrangles

SRB
85 86

square

rectangle

rhombus

trapezoid

1. A parallelogram is a quadrangle
   that has 2 pairs of parallel sides.
   Draw a parallelogram at the right.

2. Answer *yes* or *no*. Then explain your
   answers to a friend or someone at home.

   a. Is a rectangle a parallelogram? _____

   b. Is a square a parallelogram? _____

   c. Is a square a rhombus? _____

   d. Is a trapezoid a parallelogram? _____

3. Draw a quadrangle that has at least
   1 right angle.

4. Draw a quadrangle that has 2 pairs
   of equal sides but is NOT a parallelogram.

A Polygon Alphabet

Can you design an alphabet using only polygons? Try reading this message:

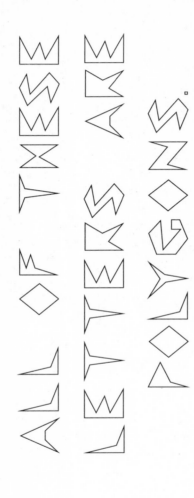

ALL OF THESE
LETTERS ARE
POLYGONS.

Now try designing your own alphabet. You can start with the samples above and finish the alphabet, or design your own versions of all 26 letters. Start with all capital letters. You'll have to simplify, because a polygon can't have any curves, and it can't have any "holes."

For example, if you look at the letter "P" in the sample above, you see that there is no opening in the upper part. Making it look like this, ⌐, would make it easier to read, but it wouldn't be a polygon!

Write the alphabet you designed on the back of this paper. When your alphabet is finished, look at all of the letters and ask yourself the following questions:

a. Which letters are convex polygons?

b. Which letters are nonconvex (concave) polygons?

c. Do any of your letters have special names as polygons?

d. Which letters were most difficult to design? Why?

Use your alphabet to write a message to someone who is not in your class. Was that person able to read it? Report back to the class.

If you enjoyed this activity, you can continue by designing the 26 lowercase (small) letters and the 10 digits, as well.

Definition Match

Match each description of a geometric figure in Column I with its name
in Column II. Some of the items in Column II don't have a match.

I

II

a. a polygon with 4 right angles and
4 sides of the same length

_____ octagon

_____ rhombus

b. a polygon with 4 sides, none of
which are the same size

_____ right angle

c. a quadrilateral with exactly one
pair of opposite sides that are
parallel

_____ trapezoid

d. lines that never intersect

_____ hexagon

_____ square

e. a parallelogram with all sides the
same length, but not a rectangle

_____ equilateral triangle

_____ perpendicular lines

f. a polygon with 8 sides

_____ parallel lines

g. a polygon with 5 sides

_____ pentagon

h. an angle that measures 90°

_____ isosceles triangle

i. a triangle with all sides the same
length

_____ quadrangle

Use with Lesson 1.6.

13

The Radius of a Circle

1. Find a circular object. Trace it in the space below.

   a. Draw a point to mark the approximate center of the circle.
   Then draw a point on the circle.

   b. Use a straightedge to draw the **radius** that connects these points.

   c. Measure the radius to the nearest $\frac{1}{4}$ inch.

   The radius of the circle is _____ inches.

2. Find another circular object. Trace it in the space below.

   a. Draw a point to mark the approximate center of the circle.
   Then draw a point on the circle.

   b. Use a straightedge to draw the **radius** that connects these points.

   c. Measure the radius to the nearest millimeter.

   The radius of the circle is _____ millimeters.

Polygon Riddles

Answer each riddle. Then draw a picture of the shape in the space to the right.

1. I am a polygon.

I am a quadrangle.

All of my sides are the same length.

None of my angles are right angles.

What am I? _____

2. I am a quadrangle.

I have two pairs of parallel sides.

All of my angles are right angles.

I am not a square.

What am I? _____

3. I am a polygon.

All of my sides have the same measure.

All of my angles have the same measure.

I have three sides.

What am I? _____

4. Make up your own polygon riddle using 4 clues. Make two of the clues hard and two of the clues easy. Ask a friend or someone at home to solve your polygon riddle.

_____

_____

_____

Unit 2: Using Numbers and Organizing Data

Your child is about to begin this year's work with numbers. Throughout the school year, the class will examine what numbers mean and how they are used in everyday life to convey information and solve problems.

In today's world, numbers are all around us—in newspapers and magazines and on TV. We use them

- to count things (*How many people are in the room?*)
- to measure things (*How tall are you?*)
- to create codes (*What is your Social Security number?*)
- to locate things in reference frames (*What time is it?*)
- to express rates, scales, and percents (*How many miles per gallon does your car get? What percent voted for Jamie?*)

The class will experience many different situations in which numbers are used. Your child will collect examples of numbers throughout the year and record the most interesting ones in a journal.

While we often deal with numbers one at a time, there are times when we need to interpret a whole collection of numbers. The class will learn to organize such collections of numbers in tables and graphs and to draw conclusions about them.

Computation is an important part of problem solving. Fortunately, we are no longer restricted to paper-and-pencil methods of computation: We can use calculators to solve lengthy problems or computer programs to solve very complex ones. Your child will have many opportunities for practicing mental and paper-and-pencil methods of computation, for using a calculator, and for deciding which is most appropriate for solving a particular problem.

Many of us were taught that there is just one way to do computations. For example, we may have learned to subtract by "borrowing." We may not have realized that there are other ways of subtracting numbers. While students will not be expected to learn more than one method, they will examine several different methods and realize that there are often several ways to arrive at the same result. They will have the option of learning a method they find most comfortable, or even inventing one of their own.

Mathematics games will be used throughout the school year to practice various arithmetic skills. Through games, practice becomes a thinking activity to be enjoyed. The games your child will play in this unit will provide practice with renaming numbers, with addition, and with subtraction. They require very little in the way of materials, so you may play them at home as well.

Please keep this Family Letter for reference as your child works through Unit 2.

Vocabulary

Important terms in Unit 2:

algorithm A set of step-by-step instructions for doing something, such as carrying out a computation or solving a problem.

base ten The property of our number system that results in each place having a value of 10 times the place to its right.

column-addition method A method for adding numbers in which the addends' digits are first added in each place-value column separately and then 10-for-1 trades are made until each column has only one digit. Lines are drawn to separate the place-value columns.

100s	10s	1s
3	2	8
2	4	8
+ 1	8	7
3	12	15
3	13	5
4	3	5

Add the columns: 3 | 12 | 15
Adjust the 1s and 10s: 3 | 13 | 5
Adjust the 10s and 100s: 4 | 3 | 5

equivalent names Different names for the same number. For example, $2 + 6$, $4 + 4$, $12 − 4$, $18 − 10$, $100 − 92$, $5 + 1 + 2$, eight, VIII, and ||||| ||| are equivalent names for 8.

line plot A sketch of data in which check marks, Xs, or other marks above a number line show the frequency of each value.

Number of Students

Number of Siblings

mean The sum of a set of numbers divided by the number of numbers in the set. The mean is often referred to simply as the *average*.

median The middle value in a set of data when the data are listed in order from least to greatest. If there is an even number of data points, the median is the *mean* of the two middle values.

mode The value or values that occur most often in a set of data.

name-collection box A diagram that is used for writing equivalent names for a number.

8
$2 + 6$
$4 + 4$
VIII
eight

partial-sums method A way to add in which sums are computed for each place (ones, tens, hundreds, and so on) separately, and are then added to give the final answer.

Example: $496 + 229 + 347 = ?$

$$
\begin{array}{r}
496 \\
229 \\
+\ 347 \\
\hline
\end{array}
$$

Add the hundreds: $400 + 200 + 300 \rightarrow 900$
Add the tens: $90 + 20 + 40 \rightarrow 150$
Add the ones: $6 + 9 + 7 \rightarrow 22$
Find the total: $900 + 150 + 22 \rightarrow 1,072$

range The difference between the maximum and the minimum in a set of data.

whole numbers The numbers 0, 1, 2, 3, 4, and so on.

Family Letter, *continued*

Do-Anytime Activities

To work with your child on the concepts taught in this unit, try these interesting and rewarding activities:

1 Have your child see how many numbers he or she can identify in newspapers, magazines, advertisements, or news broadcasts.

2 Have your child collect and compare the measurements (height and weight) or accomplishments of favorite professional athletes.

3 Look up the different time zones of the United States and the world, quizzing your child on what time it would be at that moment at a particular location.

4 Have your child look for different representations of the same number. For example, he or she may see the same money amounts expressed in different ways, such as 50¢, $0.50, or 50 cents.

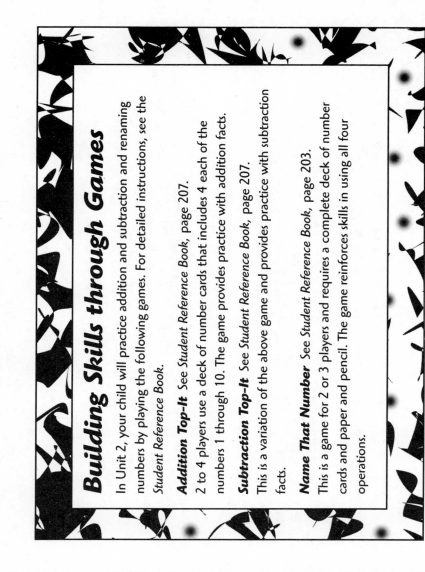

Building Skills through Games

In Unit 2, your child will practice addition and subtraction and renaming numbers by playing the following games. For detailed instructions, see the *Student Reference Book.*

Addition Top-It *See Student Reference Book,* page 207.
2 to 4 players use a deck of number cards that includes 4 each of the numbers 1 through 10. The game provides practice with addition facts.

Subtraction Top-It *See Student Reference Book,* page 207.
This is a variation of the above game and provides practice with subtraction facts.

Name That Number *See Student Reference Book,* page 203.
This is a game for 2 or 3 players and requires a complete deck of number cards and paper and pencil. The game reinforces skills in using all four operations.

As You Help Your Child with Homework

As your child brings assignments home, you may want to go over the instructions together, clarifying them as necessary. The answers listed below will guide you through some of the Study Links in this unit.

Study Link 2.2

4. Sample answers:
$10 + 10 + 10 + 10$
$100 - 60$

5. Sample answers:
18×2
$40 - 4$

Study Link 2.3

1. 876,504,000
5. a. 4,499,702   c. 30,457,300
6. a. 496,708   c. 19,410,366

Study Link 2.4

2. 581,970,000   3. 97,654,320
6. 97,308,080

Study Link 2.5

2. 27   3. 8   4. 2   5. 6   6. 5

Study Link 2.6

1. **Class Data on Computer Time**

Number
of
Students

Number of Hours
Spent on the Computer Each Week

Study Link 2.7

Sample problem using the partial-sums method:

1. 152   2. 510
3. 613   4. 1,432

	4	9	3
+	9	3	9
1	3	0	0
	1	2	0
+	1	2	
1	4	3	2

Study Link 2.8

1. a. 645   b. 19   c. 626   d. 151
2. giraffe, Asian elephant, and rhinoceros
3. 90   4. dog   5. mouse

Sample problem using the column-addition method:

7. 136   8. 720
9. 225   10. 720

	8	9
+	4	7
12	16	
13	6	
1	3	6

Study Link 2.9

Sample problem using the trade-first subtraction method:

1. 68   2. 382   3. 367

8	16	
9	6	
−	2	8
6	8	

Sample problem using the partial-differences subtraction method:

1. 29   2. 57   3. 406

8	4	
−	5	5
+	3	0
−		1
2	9	

2. a. 7   b. 0   c. 7   d. 0   e. 1
3. Answers vary.

Use with Lesson 1.9.

Numbers Everywhere

Read pages 2 and 3 in your *Student Reference Book*.

Find examples of numbers—all kinds of numbers. Look in newspapers and magazines. Look in books. Look on food packages. Ask people in your family for examples.

Write your numbers below. If an adult says you may, cut out the numbers and tape them onto the back of this page.

Be sure you write what the numbers mean.

Example Mount Everest is 29,028 feet high. It is the world's tallest mountain.

_____

_____

_____

_____

_____

_____

_____

_____

_____

_____

_____

_____

_____

_____

_____

Many Names for Numbers

SRB
131

1. Cross out the names that do not belong in the name-collection box below.

28
67 − 39
4 × 7
2 × 8
$\frac{56}{2}$
100 ÷ 4

2. Write the name for this name-collection box.

413 − 281
50 + 40 + 42
150 − 18
66 × 2
133 − 1

3. Write five names for 64.

64

4. Pretend that the 4-key is broken on your calculator. Write six ways to display the number 40 on the calculator without using the 4-key. Try to use different numbers and operations.

Example 2 × 2 × 10

_____ _____

_____ _____

5. Now pretend that the 3-key and the 6-key are broken. Write six ways to display the number 36 without using these keys.

_____ _____

_____ _____

25

Place Value in Whole Numbers

SRB 4

1. Write the number that has

6 in the millions place,
4 in the thousands place,
7 in the ten-millions place,
5 in the hundred-thousands place,
8 in the hundred-millions place, and
0 in the remaining places.

_____ , _____ , _____ .

2. Write the number that has

7 in the ten-thousands place,
3 in the millions place,
1 in the hundred-thousands place,
8 in the tens place,
2 in the ten-millions place, and
0 in the remaining places.

_____ , _____ , _____ .

3. Compare the two numbers you wrote in Problems 1 and 2.

Which is greater? _____

4. The 6 in 46,711,304 stands for 6 _*million*_, or _**6,000,000**_.

a. The 4 in 508,433,529 stands for 400 _____ , or _____ .

b. The 8 in 182,945,777 stands for 80 _____ , or _____ .

c. The 5 in 509,822,119 stands for 500 _____ , or _____ .

d. The 3 in 450,037,111 stands for 30 _____ , or _____ .

5. Write the number that is 1 million more.

a. 3,499,702 _____

b. 12,877,000 _____

c. 29,457,300 _____

d. 149,691,688 _____

6. Write the number that is 1 million less.

a. 1,496,708 _____

b. 5,321,589 _____

c. 20,410,366 _____

d. 450,620,500 _____

More Place Value in Whole Numbers

1. Write the numbers in order from smallest to largest.

15,964   1,509,460   150,094,400
1,400,960   15,094,600

_____

_____

_____

2. Write the number that has

   5 in the hundred-millions place,
   7 in the ten-thousands place,
   1 in the millions place,
   9 in the hundred-thousands place,
   8 in the ten-millions place, and
   0 in all other places.

_____ , _____ , _____

3. Write the largest number you can. Use each digit just once.

   3   5   0   7   9   2   6   4   _____

4. Write the value of the digit 8 in each numeral below.

a. 80,007,941 _____   **b.** 835,099,714 _____

c. 8,714,366 _____   **d.** 860,490 _____

5. Write each number using digits.

a. four hundred eighty-seven million, sixty-three _____

b. fifteen million, two hundred ninety-seven _____

6. Answer the following riddle:

I am an 8-digit number.

• The digit in the thousands place is the result of dividing 64 by 8.
• The digit in the millions place is the result of dividing 63 by 9.
• The digit in the ten-millions place is the result of dividing 54 by 6.
• The digit in the tens place is the result of dividing 40 by 5.
• The digit in the hundred-thousands place is the result of dividing 33 by 11.
• All the other digits are the result of subtracting any number from itself.

What number am I? _____ , _____ , _____

Collecting Data

SRB
62–66

1. Make a list of all the people in your family. Include all the people living at home now. Also include any brothers or sisters that live somewhere else. The people who live at home do not have to be related to you. Don't forget to write your name in the list.

   You will need this information to learn about the sizes of families in your class.

   Names of people in my family:

   _____   _____

   _____   _____

   _____   _____

   How many people are in your family? _____

The tally chart at the right shows the number of books that some fourth grade students read over the summer.

Use the information to answer the questions below.

Number of Books Reported	Number of Students
2	///
3	/////
4	///// //
5	///// /
6	//
7	//
8	////

2. How many students reported the

   number of books they read? _____

3. What is the **maximum** (the largest

   number of books reported)? _____

4. What is the **minimum** (the smallest

   number of books reported)? _____

5. What is the **range**? _____

6. What is the **mode** (the most frequent

   number of books reported)? _____

Line Plots

Mrs. Chen's students estimated the amount of time they spend on the computer each week. The tally chart below shows the data they collected.

Number of Hours on the Computer per Week	Number of Students
0	~~////~~ ////
1	~~////~~
2	///
3	///
4	//
5	/
6	
7	//

1. Construct a line plot for the data.

Class Data on Computer Time

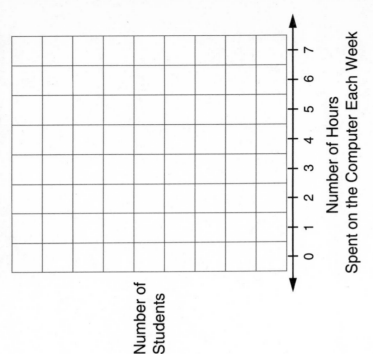

Number of
Students

0   1   2   3   4   5   6   7

Number of Hours
Spent on the Computer Each Week

2. Find the following landmarks for the data:

a. What is the maximum number of hours spent on the computer

each week? _____ hours

b. What is the minimum number of hours spent on the computer

each week? _____ hours

c. What is the range? _____ hours

d. What is the mode? _____ hours

e. What is the median number of hours spent on the computer

each week? _____ hours

3. Estimate the amount of time that you spend on the computer

each week. _____ hours

Name _____ Date _____ Time _____

Addition of Multidigit Numbers

Use the partial-sums addition method to solve Problems 1–6.

1. 67 + 85 = _____

2. _____ = 439 + 71

3. _____ = 227 + 386

4. _____ = 493 + 939

5. 732 + 1,788 = _____

6. 4,239 + 1,508 = _____

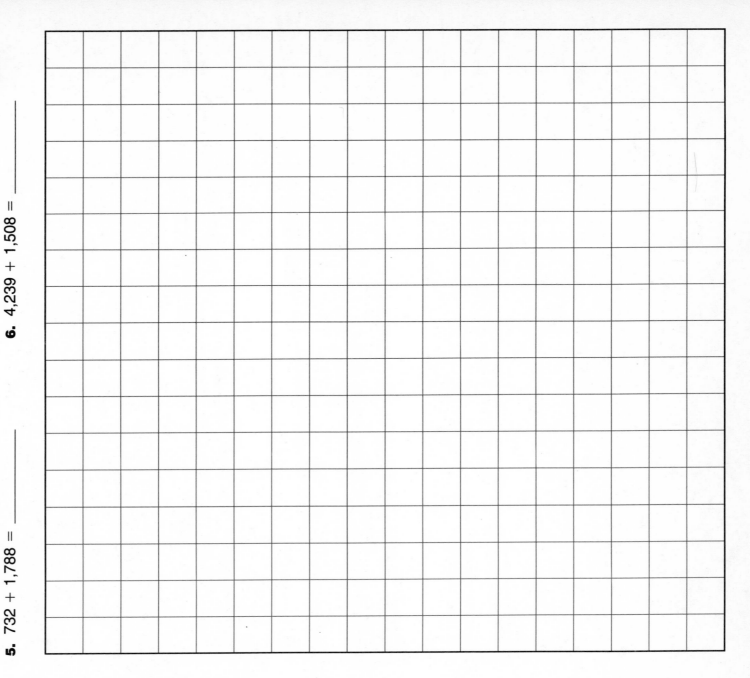

Addition of Multidigit Numbers (cont.)

Study Link 2.7

Use the column-addition method to solve Problems 7–12.

7. 89 + 47 = _____

8. _____ = 634 + 86

9. 148 + 77 = _____

10. _____ = 481 + 239

11. _____ = 746 + 827

12. 508 + 1,848 = _____

36

Gestation Period

SRB
65 66

The period between the time an animal becomes pregnant and the time its baby is born is called the **gestation period.** The table below shows the number of days in the average gestation period for some animals.

Average Gestation Period (in days)	
Animal	**Number of Days**
dog	61
giraffe	457
goat	151
human	266
Asian elephant	645
mouse	19
squirrel	44
rhinoceros	480
rabbit	31

Source: World Almanac

1. For the gestation periods listed in the table …

   a. What is the maximum number of days?

      _____ days

   b. What is the minimum number of days?

      _____ days

   c. What is the range (the difference between the maximum and the minimum)?

      _____ days

   d. What is the median (middle number of days)?

      _____ days

2. Which animals have an average gestation period that is longer than 1 year?

   _____

3. How much longer is the average gestation period for a goat than for a dog?

   _____ days

4. Which animal has an average gestation period that is about twice as long as a rabbit's? _____

5. Which animal has an average gestation period that is about half as long as a squirrel's? _____

Use with Lesson 2.8.

Subtraction of Multidigit Numbers

Use the trade-first subtraction method to solve the problems.

1. $96 - 28 = $ _____

2. _____ $= 469 - 87$

3. _____ $= 732 - 365$

4. $4,321 - 75 = $ _____

5. $5,613 - 2,724 = $ _____

6. _____ $= 600 - 438$

Subtraction of Multidigit Numbers (cont.)

Use the partial-differences subtraction method to solve the problems.

1. _____ = 84 − 55

2. 136 − 79 = _____

3. _____ = 573 − 167

4. _____ = 506 − 282

5. _____ = 5,673 − 1,194

6. 3,601 − 1,063 = _____

Family Letter

Unit 3: Multiplication and Division; Number Sentences and Algebra

One of our goals in the coming weeks is to finish memorizing the multiplication facts for single-digit numbers. To help students master the facts, they will play several math games. Ask your child to teach you one of the games described in his or her *Student Reference Book*, and play a few rounds together. The class will also take a series of 50-facts tests. Because correct answers are counted only up to the first mistake (and not counted thereafter), your child may at first receive a low score. If this happens, don't be alarmed. Before long, scores will improve dramatically. Help your child set a realistic goal for the next test, and discuss what can be done to meet that goal.

Your child will use Multiplication/Division Fact Triangles to review the relationship between multiplication and division. (For example, $4 \times 5 = 20$, and so $20 \div 5 = 4$ and $20 \div 4 = 5$.) Fact Triangles can also serve as flash cards. You can use the triangles to quiz your child on the basic facts and test your child's progress.

In this unit, alternative symbols for multiplication and division are introduced. An asterisk (*) may be substituted for the traditional × symbol, as in $4 * 5 = 20$. A slash (/) may be used in place of the traditional ÷ symbol, as in $20 / 4 = 5$.

In Unit 3, the class will continue the World Tour, a yearlong project in which the students travel to a number of different countries. Their first flight will take them to Cairo, Egypt. These travels serve as background for many interesting activities in which students look up numerical information, analyze this information, and solve problems.

Finally, the class will have its first formal introduction to solving equations in algebra. (Informal activities with missing numbers in number stories have been built into the program since first grade.) Formal introduction to algebra in fourth grade may surprise you, since algebra is usually regarded as a high school subject. However, an early start in algebra is integral to the *Everyday Mathematics* philosophy.

Please keep this Family Letter for reference as your child works through Unit 3.

Use with Lesson 2.10.

Vocabulary

Important terms in Unit 3:

change diagram A diagram used in *Everyday Mathematics* to represent situations in which quantities are increased or decreased.

Start	Change	End
14	−5	9

comparison diagram A diagram used in *Everyday Mathematics* to represent situations in which two quantities are compared.

Quantity	
12	
Quantity	Difference
9	?

dividend In division, the number that is being divided. For example, in 35 ÷ 5 = 7, the dividend is 35.

divisor In division, the number that divides another number. For example, in 35 ÷ 5 = 7, the divisor is 5.

Fact Triangle A triangular flash card labeled with the numbers of a fact family that students can use to practice addition/subtraction or multiplication/division facts.

factor One of two or more numbers that are multiplied to give a product. The numbers multiplied are called *factors* of the *product*. For example, 4 and 3 are factors of 12, because 4 * 3 = 12.

Family Letter, *continued*

number sentence A sentence that is made up of at least two numbers or expressions and a relation symbol (=, >, <, ≥, ≤, or ≠). Most number sentences also contain at least one operation symbol (+, −, ×, *, ·, ÷, /). Number sentences may also have grouping symbols, such as parentheses.

open sentence A *number sentence* in which one or more *variables* hold the places of missing numbers. For example, 5 + x = 13 is an open sentence.

parts-and-total diagram A diagram used in *Everyday Mathematics* to represent situations in which two or more quantities are combined.

Total		
?		
Part	Part	Part
9	10	9

Total	
30	
Part	Part
12	18

percent Per hundred, or out of a hundred. For example, "48% of the students in the school are boys" means that 48 out of every 100 students in the school are boys.

product The result of multiplying two numbers called *factors*. For example, in 4 * 3 = 12, the product is 12.

quotient The result of dividing one number by another. For example, in 35 ÷ 5 = 7, the quotient is 7.

square number A number that is the product of a whole number multiplied by itself. For example, 25 is a square number because 25 = 5 * 5. The square numbers are 1, 4, 9, 16, 25, and so on.

variable A letter or other symbol that represents a number. A variable can represent one specific number or it can stand for many different number.

Use with Lesson 2.10.

Family Letter, *continued*

Do-Anytime Activities

To work with your child on the concepts taught in this unit, try these interesting and rewarding activities:

1 Continue work on multiplication and division facts by using Fact Triangles and fact families or by playing games described in the *Student Reference Book.*

2 As the class proceeds through the unit, give your child multidigit addition and subtraction problems related to the lessons covered, such as $348 + 29$, $427 + 234$, $72 - 35$, and $815 - 377$.

3 Help your child recognize and identify real-world examples of right angles, such as the corner of a book, and examples of parallel lines, such as railroad tracks.

Building Skills through Games

Baseball Multiplication   *See Student Reference Book, pages 186 and 187.*
Two players will need 4 regular dice, 4 pennies, and a calculator to play this game. Practicing the multiplication facts for 1–12 and strengthening mental arithmetic skills are the goals of *Baseball Multiplication.*

Beat the Calculator   *See Student Reference Book, page 188.*
This game involves 3 players and requires a calculator and a deck of number cards with 4 each of the numbers 1 through 10. Playing *Beat the Calculator* helps your child review basic multiplication facts.

Broken Calculator   *See Student Reference Book, page 189.*
This game reinforces skills in using the four operations as your child tries to display a given number on a calculator without the use of a "broken" key.

Division Arrays   *See Student Reference Book, page 194.*
Materials for this game include number cards, 1 each of the numbers 6 through 18; a regular (6-sided) die; 18 counters; and paper and pencil. This game, involving 2 to 4 players, reinforces the idea of dividing objects into equal groups.

Multiplication Top-It   *See Student Reference Book, page 208.*
The game can be played with 2 to 4 players and requires a deck of cards with 4 each of the numbers 1 through 10. This game helps your child review basic multiplication facts.

Name That Number   *See Student Reference Book, page 203.*
Played with 2 or 3 players, this game requires a complete deck of number cards and paper and pencil. Your child tries to name a target number by adding, subtracting, multiplying, and dividing the numbers on as many of the cards as possible.

Use with Lesson 2.10.

As You Help Your Child with Homework

As your child brings assignments home, you may want to go over the instructions together, clarifying them as necessary. The answers listed below will guide you through some of the Study Links in this unit.

Study Link 3.2

1. 24
2. 54
3. 28
4. 16
5. 45
6. 18
7. 40
8. 25
9. 48

Study Link 3.3

1. 6
2. 8
3. 6
4. 3
6. 20; 5
7. 18; 6
8. 49; 7
9. 9; 2
10. 7; 5
11. 7; 4
12. 3; 9
13. 6; 6

Study Link 3.4

1. 5
2. 7
3. 72
4. 10
5. 32

Answers vary for Problems 6–14.

Study Link 3.5

1. 4
2. 3,360
3. Answers vary.
4. a. less   b. less
5. false
6. 134,950

Study Link 3.6

Cities	Measurement on Map (inches)	Real Distance (miles)
Cape Town and Durban	4 inches	800 miles
Durban and Pretoria	1¾ inches	350 miles
Cape Town and Johannesburg	4 inches	800 miles
Johannesburg and Queensburg	2 inches	400 miles
East London and Upington	2½ inches	500 miles
_____ and _____	Answers vary.	

Study Link 3.7

1. 659 − 457 = 202
2. 1,545 + 2,489 = 4,034
3. 700 − 227 = 473
4. 939 + 2,657 = 3,596
5. 624 + 470 + 336 = 1,430

Study Link 3.8

1. F
2. F
3. T
4. T
5. F
6. T
7. T
8. ?
9. Sample answers: 25 + 20 < 30; 150 + 250 > 300
10. Sample answers: 25 / 5 = 5; 158 − 52 = 100
11. a. There is not a relation symbol such as = , >, or <.
    b. Sample answer: 7 * 8 = 56
    c. Sample answer: 7 * 8 = 49

Study Link 3.9

1. 33
2. 27
3. 1
4. 24
5. 37
6. 8
7. 3 * (6 + 4) = 30
8. 15 = (20 − 7) + 2
9. 7 + (7 * 3) = 4 * 7
10. 9 * 6 = (25 * 2) + 4
11. 72 / 9 = (2 * 3) + 18 / 9
12. 35 / (42 / 6) = (10 − 6) + 1
13. T
14. ?
15. F
16. F
17. T
18. ?

Study Link 3.11

1. Logic Grid

	Red	Yellow	Blue
Rafael	✓	✗	✗
Adena	✗	✗	✓
Jordana	✗	✓	✗

Rafael: red   Adena: blue   Jordana: yellow

2. Logic Grid

Pizza	Hamburger	Hot Dog	Macaroni and Cheese
Mike	✓	✗	✗	✗
Laura	✗	✓	✗	✗
Fred	✗	✗	✓	✗
Liz	✗	✗	✗	✓

Mike: pizza   Laura: hamburger
Fred: hot dog   Liz: macaroni and cheese

Use with Lesson 2.10.

Multiplication Facts

SRB
125 126

Complete the Multiplication/Division Facts Table below.

*, /	1	2	3	4	5	6	7	8	9	10
1						6				
2										
3	3		9							
4		8								
5										
6										
7		14								
8										
9										
10										

Name

Date

Time

Fact Triangles

Study Link
3.2

Complete these Multiplication/Division Fact Triangles.

1.

2.

3.

4.

5.

6.

7.

8.

9.

Mystery Numbers

SRB
258

Find the mystery numbers.

1. I am thinking of a mystery number. If I multiply it
by 4, the answer is 24. What is the mystery number? _____

2. I am thinking of another number. If I multiply it
by 3, the answer is 24. What is the number? _____

3. I multiplied a number by itself and got 36.
What number did I multiply by itself? _____

4. If I multiply 7 by a number, I get 21.
What number did I use? _____

Write your own mystery number problem.

5. _____

_____

_____

Fill in the missing numbers.

6. 4 * 5 = _____

_____ * 4 = 20

7. _____ = 6 * 3

18 = _____ * 3

8. 7 * 7 = _____

_____ * 7 = 49

9. _____ * 2 = 18

18 = _____ * 9

10. 35 = _____ * 5

_____ * 7 = 35

11. 28 = _____ * 4

_____ * 7 = 28

12. _____ * 9 = 27

27 = _____ * 3

13. _____ * 6 = 36

6 * _____ = 36

Missing Numbers

Equivalents

3 * 4	12 / 3	12 ÷ 3	3 < 5 (< means "is less than")
3 × 4	$\frac{12}{3}$	3)12	5 > 3 (> means "is greater than")

Complete each fact by filling in the missing numbers.
Use the Multiplication/Division Facts Table to help you.

1. 30 / 6 = _____   **2.** 21 / _____ = 3

3. 9 = _____ ÷ 8   **4.** 100 / _____ = 10

5. _____ / 4 = 8   **6.** 25 ÷ _____ =

7. _____ = 42 /   **8.** 8 / _____ =

9. 4 = _____ /   **10.** _____ ÷ _____ = 1

11. _____ / 2 = _____   **12.** 10 * _____ =

Challenge

13. 5 * _____ * _____ = 30   **14.** 54 = _____ * _____ * _____

*, /	1	2	3	4	5	6	7	8	9	10
1	1	2	3	4	5	6	7	8	9	10
2	2	4	6	8	10	12	14	16	18	20
3	3	6	9	12	15	18	21	24	27	30
4	4	8	12	16	20	24	28	32	36	40
5	5	10	15	20	25	30	35	40	45	50
6	6	12	18	24	30	36	42	48	54	60
7	7	14	21	28	35	42	49	56	63	70
8	8	16	24	32	40	48	56	64	72	80
9	9	18	27	36	45	54	63	72	81	90
10	10	20	30	40	50	60	70	80	90	100

Name

Date

Time

Number Stories about Egypt

Study Link 3.5

SRB
149

1. The area of Egypt is about 386,700 square miles. The area of Wyoming is about 97,818 square miles. About how many times larger is Egypt than Wyoming?

About _____ times larger

2. The Nile is the longest river in the world. It is about 4,160 miles long. The Huang River is the fourth longest river in the world. It is about 800 miles shorter than the Nile. About how long is the Huang River?

About _____ miles

3. The Suez Canal links the Mediterranean and Red Seas. It is 103 miles long and was opened in 1869. For how many years has the Suez Canal been open?

_____ years

4. a. Aswan, Egypt, is the driest inhabited place in the world. The average annual rainfall is 0.02 inch. Is this more or less than $\frac{1}{4}$ inch per year?

_____

b. Minya el Qamn, Egypt, is the sixth driest inhabited place in the world. The average annual rainfall is 0.20 inch. Is this more or less than $\frac{1}{4}$ inch per year?

_____

5. The population of Cairo, Egypt, is about 6,789,000. Lagos, Nigeria, is the most populated city in Africa, with 10,287,000 people. True or false: There are about 5 million more people living in Lagos than in Cairo.

_____

6. There are about 2,950 miles of railroad in Egypt. There are about 137,900 miles of railroad in the United States. About how many fewer miles of railroad are there in Egypt than in the United States?

About _____ miles

Use with Lesson 3.5.

53

Map Scale

Here is a map of South Africa. Use a ruler to measure the shortest distance between cities. Use the map scale to convert these measurements to real distances.

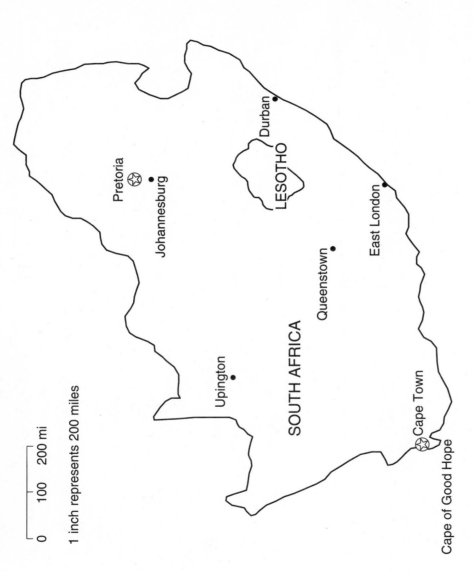

0   100   200 mi

1 inch represents 200 miles

Cities	Measurement on Map (inches)	Real Distance (miles)
Cape Town and Durban		
Durban and Pretoria		
Cape Town and Johannesburg		
Johannesburg and Queenstown		
East London and Upington		
_____ and _____		

Use with Lesson 3.6.

55

Addition and Subtraction Number Stories

1. In 1896, the United Kingdom had the largest navy in the world with 659 ships. France had the second-largest navy with 457 ships. The United States was tenth with only 95 ships. How many more ships did the United Kingdom have than France?

_____
(number model)

Answer: _____ more ships

2. Rhode Island, the smallest state in the United States, has an area of 1,545 square miles. The area of the second-smallest state, Delaware, is 2,489 square miles. What is the combined area of these two states?

_____
(number model)

Answer: _____ square miles

3. A polar bear can weigh as much as 700 kilograms. An American black bear can weigh as much as 227 kilograms. How much more can a polar bear weigh than an American black bear?

_____
(number model)

Answer: _____ kilograms more

4. The Cat Fancier's Association registered 939 Burmese cats and 2,657 Siamese cats in 1997. How many Burmese and Siamese cats were registered?

_____
(number model)

Answer: _____ cats

5. According to the National Register of Historic Places, New York City has the greatest number of historic places in the United States with 624 sites. Philadelphia is second with 470 sites and Washington, D.C., is third with 336 sites. In all, how many historic sites are there in the top three cities?

_____
(number model)

Answer: _____ historic sites

Use with Lesson 3.7.

True, False, and "Can't Tell" Number Sentences

Next to each number sentence, write "T" if it is true, "F" if it is false, or "?" if you can't tell.

1. 20 − 12 = 8 * 3 _____

2. 7 = 14 * 2 _____

3. 497 < 500 _____

4. 16 / 4 = 4 _____

5. 15 + 10 = 5 _____

6. 24 > 11 + 11 _____

7. 100 − 5 = 95 _____

8. 33 − 4 _____

9. Write two true number sentences.

_____

_____

10. Write two false number sentences.

_____

_____

11. a. Explain why 7 * 8 is not a number sentence.

_____

_____

b. How could you change 7 * 8 to make a true number sentence?

_____

c. How could you change 7 * 8 to make a false number sentence?

_____

Parentheses in Number Sentences

Make each of the following a true sentence by filling in the missing number.

1. 9 + (4 * 6) = _____

2. (45 / 5) * 3 = _____

3. (20 / 4) / 5 = _____

4. _____ = (33 − 25) * 3

5. _____ = (25 / 5) + (8 * 4)

6. (33 + 7) / (3 + 2) = _____

Make each of the following a true sentence by inserting parentheses.

7. 3 * 6 + 4 = 30

8. 15 = 20 − 7 + 2

9. 7 + 7 * 3 = 4 * 7

10. 9 * 6 = 25 * 2 + 4

11. 72 / 9 = 2 * 3 + 18 / 9

12. 35 / 42 / 6 = 10 − 6 + 1

For each of the following, write "T" if it is true, "F" if it is false, or "?" if you can't tell.

13. (4 * 6) + 13 = 47 − 10 _____

14. (3 * 7) / (15 − 12) _____

15. 15 > (7 * 6) * (10 − 9) _____

16. 30 = 1 + (4 * 6) _____

17. 20 < (64 / 8) * (12 / 4) _____

18. (6 * 5) / 3 _____

Review

SRB
128

Solve the problems.
When you've finished,
show them to someone
at home or to a
classmate. The
answers to some of
the problems are given
at the bottom of the
page for you to check yourself.

Equivalents		
3 * 4	12 / 3	12 ÷ 3
		3 < 5
		(< means "is less than")
3 × 4	$\frac{12}{3}$	$3\overline{)12}$
		5 > 3
		(> means "is greater than")

Tell whether the number sentence is true or false.

1. 35 = 7 * 5 _____

2. 43 > 34 _____

3. 25 + 25 < 50 _____

4. 49 − (7 × 7) = 0 _____

Make a true number sentence by filling in the missing number.

5. _____ = 12 / (3 + 3)

6. (60 − 28) / 4 = _____

7. (3 × 8) ÷ 6 = _____

8. 30 − (4 + 6) = _____

Make a true number sentence by inserting parentheses.

9. 4 * 2 + 10 = 18

10. 16 = 16 − 8 * 2

11. 27 / 9 / 3 = 1

12. 27 / 9 / 3 = 9

Find the solution of each open sentence below. Write a number sentence with the
solution in place of the variable. Check to see whether the number sentence is true.

Example: 6 + x = 14   *Solution:* 8   *Number sentence:* 6 + 8 = 14

Open sentence	Solution	Number sentence
13. 12 + x = 32	_____	_____
14. s = 200 − 3	_____	_____
15. 5 * y = 40	_____	_____
16. 7 = x / 4	_____	_____

1. true   **3.** false   **5.** 2   **7.** 4   **9.** (4 * 2) + 10 = 18   **11.** (27 / 9) / 3 = 1   **13.** 20   **15.** 8

Use with Lesson 3.10.

Logic Problems

SRB
149

1. Rafael, Adena, and Jordana each have a different favorite color.

   • Rafael's favorite color can be mixed with blue to make purple.

   • Adena doesn't like colors that can be found on traffic lights.

   • Jordana likes to eat bananas because they are her favorite color.

   Logic Grid

	Red	Yellow	Blue
Rafael			
Adena			
Jordana			

   What is each person's favorite color?

   Rafael _____   Adena _____   Jordana _____

2. Fred, Laura, Mike, and Liz all have a favorite type of food. Each one has a different favorite food.

   • Laura's favorite food usually comes with a bun.

   • Fred does not like food with cheese.

   • Fred's favorite food comes in a foot-long size, and he puts mustard and catsup on it.

   • Mike likes cheese, sausage, and pepperoni toppings on his favorite food.

   Logic Grid

	Pizza	Hamburger	Hot Dog	Macaroni and Cheese
Mike				
Laura				
Fred				
Liz				

   What is each person's favorite food?

   Mike _____   Laura _____

   Fred _____   Liz _____

Family Letter

Unit 4: Decimals and Their Uses

In previous grades, your child had many experiences with amounts of money written in decimal notation. In the next unit, the class will learn about other uses of decimals.

Decimals are needed because numerical information often cannot be expressed by a whole number—it may be a quantity between two whole numbers.

The class will focus on a number of examples of uses of decimals in everyday life. For example, a small thermometer for taking body temperatures usually has marks that are spaced $\frac{2}{10}$ of a degree apart. This allows for very accurate measurements of body temperature.

Normal body temperature is about 98.6 °F.

Students will explore how decimals are used in measuring distances, times, and gasoline mileage. If you have a car, your child will also calculate the average number of miles your car can travel on 1 gallon of gasoline. Your assistance will be needed to complete this project.

We will also begin a yearlong measurement routine. Students will find their very own "personal references," which they will use to estimate lengths, heights, and distances in metric units. For example, your child might discover that the distance from the base of his or her thumb to the tip of his or her index finger is about 10 centimeters and then use this fact to estimate the width of this page to be about 20 centimeters.

About 10 cm

The World Tour will continue. Small groups of students will work together to gather information about different countries in Africa and then share what they have learned with the rest of the class. This will provide an opportunity for students to compare and interpret data for a large number of countries from the same region.

Please keep this Family Letter for reference as your child works through Unit 4.

Vocabulary

Important terms in Unit 4:

centimeter (cm) In the metric system, a unit of length equivalent to $\frac{1}{100}$ of a meter; 10 millimeters; $\frac{1}{10}$ of a decimeter.

decimeter (dm) In the metric system, a unit of length equivalent to $\frac{1}{10}$ of a meter; 10 centimeters.

hundredths The place-value position in which a digit has a value equal to $\frac{1}{100}$ of itself; the second digit to the right of the decimal point.

meter (m) In the metric system, the fundamental unit of length from which other units of length are derived. One meter is the distance light will travel in a vacuum (empty space) in $\frac{1}{299,792,458}$ second.

millimeter (mm) In the metric system, a unit of length equivalent to $\frac{1}{1,000}$ of a meter; $\frac{1}{10}$ of a centimeter.

ONE Same as whole. See *whole.*

ones The place-value position in which a digit has a value equal to the digit itself.

personal measurement reference A convenient approximation for a standard unit of measurement. For example, many people have thumbs that are approximately one inch wide.

place value A system that values a digit according to its position or place in a number. Each place has a value ten times that of the place to its right and one-tenth of the value of the place to its left. For example, in the number 456, the 4 is in the hundreds place and has a value of 400.

tens The place-value position in which a digit has a value equal to ten times itself.

tenths The place-value position in which a digit has a value equal to $\frac{1}{10}$ of itself; the first digit to the right of the decimal point.

thousandths The place-value position in which a digit has a value equal to $\frac{1}{1,000}$ of itself; the third digit to the right of the decimal point.

whole (or ONE or unit) The entire object, collection of objects, or quantity being considered; the ONE; the unit; 100%.

1,000s	100s	10s	1s	.	0.1s	0.01s	0.001s
Thousands	Hundreds	Tens	Ones	.	Tenths	Hundredths	Thousandths

Family Letter, *continued*

Do-Anytime Activities

To work with your child on the concepts taught in this unit, try these interesting and rewarding activities:

1 Have your child track the sports statistics of a favorite athlete. Discuss the use of decimals in the statistics he or she finds.

2 Have your child compare prices of items in the supermarket.

3 Help your child create and use new personal reference measures.

4 Together, find statistics about countries in the World Tour. Look in newspapers and almanacs.

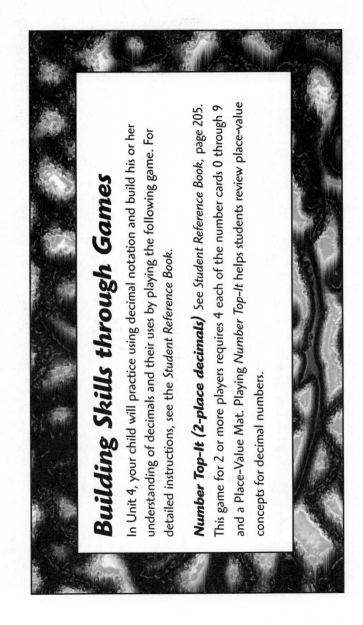

Building Skills through Games

In Unit 4, your child will practice using decimal notation and build his or her understanding of decimals and their uses by playing the following game. For detailed instructions, see the *Student Reference Book.*

Number Top-It (2-place decimals) See *Student Reference Book*, page 205. This game for 2 or more players requires 4 each of the number cards 0 through 9 and a Place-Value Mat. Playing *Number Top-It* helps students review place-value concepts for decimal numbers.

As You Help Your Child with Homework

Family Letter, *continued*

As your child brings assignments home, you may want to go over the instructions together, clarifying them as necessary. The answers listed below will guide you through some of the Study Links in this unit.

Study Link 4.2

1. | S | L | I | P | P | E | R | S |
   |---|---|---|---|---|---|---|---|

2. | B | O | B | | H | O | P |
   |---|---|---|---|---|---|---|

3. | T | H | E | | L | E | T | T | E | R | | M |
   |---|---|---|---|---|---|---|---|---|---|---|---|

Study Link 4.3

1. Seikan and Channel Tunnel
2. Between 90 and 120 miles
3. About 20 miles
4. About 12 miles
5. About 8 miles

Study Link 4.4

1. 5.18
2. 0.03
3. 120.41
4. 1.46
5. >
6. <
7. >
8. >
9. $7.37
10. $6.48

Study Link 4.5

1. a. $0.76   b. $2.43   c. $4.64   d. $2.95
2. $16.40   3. $2.57   4. $7.32
5. $18.10   6. $10.78

Study Link 4.6

1. $\frac{335}{1,000}$ 0.335
   $\frac{7}{100}$ 0.07
3. $\frac{301}{1,000}$ 0.301
   $1\frac{5}{100}$ 1.05
5. 0.346
7. 0.003
9. 0.536
11. 7.008
13. >   14. >   15. <   16. <
6. 0.092
8. 2.7
10. 0.23
12. 0.4

Study Link 4.7

1. About 7 cm; 0.07 m   2. About 12 cm; 0.12 m
3. About 4 cm; 0.04 m   4. About 6 cm; 0.06 m
5. About 2 cm; 0.02 m   6. About 14 cm; 0.14 m

Study Link 4.8

1. Answers vary.   2. 180   3. 4
4. 3,000   5. 400   6. 7
7. 460   8. 794   9. 4.5
10. 0.23   11. 60

Study Link 4.9

2. 64.8 mm   6.48 cm
3. 0.5 mm   0.05 cm
4. 19.0 mm   1.9 cm
5. 18.5 mm   1.85 cm
6. 5.0 mm   0.5 cm

Study Link 4.10

1. six thousand, eight hundred fifty-four

1,000s	100s	10s	1s
6	8	5	4

2. two and nine hundred fifty-nine thousandths

100s	10s	1s		0.1s	0.01s	0.001s
		2	.	9	5	9

3. seventy-three and four thousandths

10s	1s		0.1s	0.01s	0.001s
7	3	.	0	0	4

Decimals All Around

Find examples of decimals in newspapers, in magazines, in books, or on food packages. Ask people in your family for examples.

Write your numbers below or, if an adult says you may, cut them out and tape them on this page. Be sure to write what the numbers mean. For example: "The body temperature of a hibernating dormouse may go down to 35.6°F."

_____

_____

_____

_____

_____

_____

_____

_____

_____

_____

_____

_____

_____

_____

_____

_____

_____

_____

_____

Silly Decimal Riddles

Put the letters in the correct boxes to answer the riddles.

Example In Problem 1, the letter L goes with 0.33. Since 0.33 is between
0.25 and 0.5, put the letter L in the second box.

1. What kind of clothing can you make out of banana peels?

	L							

0.0   0.25   0.5   0.75   1   1.25   1.5   1.75   2

L	0.33	P	1.01	S	0.1
R	1.6	S	1.99	P	0.8
I	0.7	E	1.33		

2. What frog was a famous comedian?

0   $\frac{1}{4}$ $\frac{1}{2}$ $\frac{3}{4}$ 1 $1\frac{1}{4}$ $1\frac{1}{2}$ $1\frac{3}{4}$ 2

P	1.66	O	1.3
H	1.01	B	0.60
O	0.3	B	0.01

3. What's once in every minute, twice in every moment, but not once in a
thousand years?

0.0   0.1   0.2   0.3   0.4   0.5   0.6   0.7   0.8   0.9   1.0   1.1   1.2

T	0.67	R	0.99	E	0.55
T	0.05	M	1.15	E	0.88
T	$\frac{3}{4}$	E	$\frac{1}{4}$		
L	0.49	H	0.101		

Railroad Tunnel Lengths

The table below shows the five longest railroad tunnels in the world.

Tunnel	Location	Year Completed	Length in Miles
Seikan	Japan	1988	33.49
Channel Tunnel	France/England	1994	31.03
Moscow Metro	Russia	1979	19.07
London Underground	United Kingdom	1939	17.30
Dai-Shimizu	Japan	1982	13.78

Source: The Top Ten of Everything 2000

Use estimation to answer the following questions. Do not work the problems on paper or with a calculator.

1. Which two tunnels have a combined length of about 60 miles?

   _____

2. Circle the best estimate for the combined length of all five tunnels.

   a. Less than 90 miles   **b.** Between 90 and 120 miles

   c. Between 120 and 150 miles   **d.** More than 150 miles

3. About how many miles longer is the Seikan tunnel than the Dai-Shimizu tunnel?

   About _____ miles

4. About how many miles longer is the Channel Tunnel than the Moscow Metro tunnel?

   About _____ miles

Challenge

5. The Cascade tunnel in Washington state is the longest railroad tunnel in the United States. It is about $\frac{1}{4}$ the length of the Seikan. About how long is the Cascade tunnel?

   About _____ miles

Addition and Subtraction of Decimals

Add or subtract.

1. $9.87 - 4.69 =$ _____

2. $0.4 - 0.37 =$ _____

3. $96.45 + 23.96 =$ _____

4. $1.06 + 0.4 =$ _____

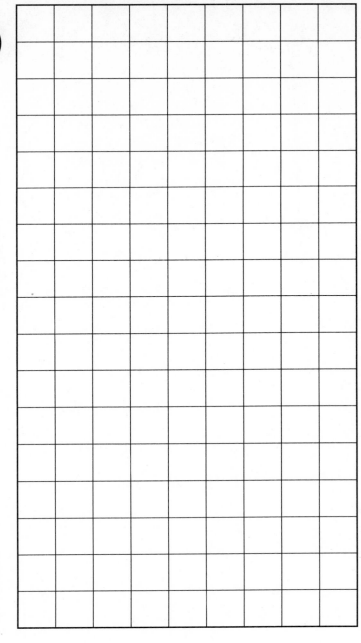

Write $<$, $>$, or $=$ to make each statement true.

5. $2.78 + 9.1$ _____ $3.36 + 8.49$

6. $0.08 + 0.97$ _____ $1.04 + 0.03$

7. $13.62 - 4.9$ _____ $9.4 - 1.33$

8. $9.4 - 5.6$ _____ $8.3 - 4.7$

Solve.

9. Cleo went to the store to buy school supplies. She bought a notebook for $2.39, a pen for $0.99, and a set of markers for $3.99. How much money did she spend in all?

_____

10. Nicholas went to the store with a $20 bill. His groceries cost $13.52. How much change did he get?

_____

Use with Lesson 4.4.

Grocery Prices—Now and Future

The table below shows some USDA grocery prices for the year 2000 and estimates of grocery prices for the year 2025.

Grocery Item	Price in 2000	Estimated Price in 2025
dozen eggs	$1.02	$1.78
loaf of white bread	$0.88	$3.31
pound of butter	$2.72	$7.36
gallon of milk	$2.70	$5.65

1. How much more is each item predicted to cost in 2025?

   a. eggs _____

   b. bread _____

   c. butter _____

   d. milk _____

2. The year is 2000. You buy bread and butter. You hand the cashier a $20 bill. How much change should you receive?

   _____

3. The year is 2025. You buy eggs and milk. You hand the cashier a $10 bill. How much change should you receive?

   _____

4. The year is 2000. You buy all 4 items. What is the total cost? _____

5. The year is 2025. You buy all 4 items. What is the total cost? _____

6. If the predictions are correct, how much more will you pay in 2025 for the 4 items than you paid in 2000?

   _____

Tenths, Hundredths, and Thousandths

Complete the table. The big cube is the ONE.

Base-10 Blocks	Fraction Notation	Decimal Notation
1.		
2.		
3.		
4.		

Write each number in decimal notation.

5. $\frac{346}{1,000}$ _____

6. $\frac{92}{1,000}$ _____

7. $\frac{3}{1,000}$ _____

8. $2\frac{7}{10}$ _____

Write each of the following in decimal notation.

9. 536 thousandths _____

10. 23 hundredths _____

11. 7 and 8 thousandths _____

12. 4 tenths _____

Write < or >.

13. 0.407 _____ 0.074

14. 0.65 _____ 0.437

15. 0.672 _____ 0.7

16. 2.38 _____ 2.4

Measuring in Centimeters

SRB
108 109

Measure each line segment to the nearest centimeter. Record the measurement in centimeters and meters.

Example

About ___5___ centimeters   About __0.05__ meter

1.

About _____ centimeters   About _____ meter

2.

About _____ centimeters   About _____ meter

3.

About _____ centimeters   About _____ meter

4.

About _____ centimeters   About _____ meter

5.

About _____ centimeters   About _____ meter

6.

About _____ centimeters   About _____ meter

Metric Measurements

SRB
109 110

1. Use your personal references to estimate the lengths of 4 objects in metric units. Then measure each object. Record your estimates and measurements.

Object	Estimated Length	Actual Length

Complete.

2. 18 cm = _____ mm

3. _____ cm = 40 mm

4. 3 m = _____ mm

5. 4 m = _____ cm

6. _____ m = 700 cm

7. 4.6 m = _____ cm

8. 7.94 m = _____ cm

9. _____ m = 450 cm

10. _____ m = 23 cm

11. 0.6 m = _____ cm

The Invention of the Meter

In 1790, the meter was defined as $\frac{1}{10,000,000}$ (one ten-millionth) of the distance from the North Pole to the equator along the meridian near Dunkerque, France, and Barcelona, Spain. The true distance along the meridian from the North Pole to the equator has been found to be 10,002,000 meters—only a 0.02% difference from the 200-year-old measurement.

Source: World Book Encyclopedia

Use with Lesson 4.8.

Rainfall Measurements

SRB
34 65 109

The table below shows the average annual rainfall for the 10 driest inhabited places in the world.

1. Fill in the missing measurements in the table.

Location	Average Annual Rainfall (mm)	Average Annual Rainfall (cm)
Aswan, Egypt	0.5	0.05
Luxor, Egypt	0.7	
Arica, Chile	1.1	
Ica, Peru	2.3	
Antofagasta, Chile	4.9	
Minya el Qamn, Egypt		0.51
Asyut, Egypt	5.2	
Callao, Peru	12.0	
Trujillo, Peru		1.4
Fayyum, Egypt	19.0	

Source: The Top Ten of Everything 2000

For each of the questions below, record the measurement in both millimeters and centimeters.

2. What is the total annual rainfall of the 10 driest places? _____ mm _____ cm

3. What is the minimum average annual rainfall? _____ mm _____ cm

4. What is the maximum average annual rainfall? _____ mm _____ cm

5. What is the range of average annual rainfall? _____ mm _____ cm

6. What is the median average rainfall? _____ mm _____ cm

Use with Lesson 4.9.

Place-Value Puzzles

Study Link 4.10

SRB 28 29

Use the clues to write the digits in the boxes and find each number. Then write the number in words on the line below the problem. For example, for 345, you would write *three hundred forty-five.*

1,000s	100s	10s	1s

1.
- Write 5 in the tens place.
- Find $\frac{1}{2}$ of 24. Subtract 4. Write the result in the hundreds place.
- Add 7 to the digit in the tens place. Divide by 2. Write the result in the thousands place.
- In the ones place, write an even number greater than 2 that has not been used yet.

Answer (in words):

100s	10s	1s	0.1s	0.01s	0.001s
		.			

2.
- Divide 15 by 3. Write the result in the hundredths place.
- Multiply 2 by 10. Divide by 10. Write the result in the ones place.
- Write a digit in the tenths place that is 4 more than the digit in the hundredths place.
- Add 7 to the digit in the ones place. Write the result in the thousandths place.

Answer (in words):

10s	1s	0.1s	0.01s	0.001s
	.			

3.
- Write the result of 6 * 9 divided by 18 in the ones place.
- Double 8. Divide by 4. Write the result in the thousandths place.
- Add 3 to the digit in the thousandths place. Write the result in the tens place.
- Write the same digit in the tenths and hundredths places so that the sum of all the digits is 14.

Answer (in words):

Family Letter

Unit 5: Big Numbers, Estimation, and Computation

In this unit, your child will begin to multiply 1- and 2-digit numbers using what we call the **partial-products method**. In preparation for this, students will learn to play the game *Multiplication Wrestling*. Ask your child to explain the rules to you and play an occasional game together. While students are expected to learn the partial-products method, they will also investigate the **lattice multiplication method**, which students have often enjoyed in the past.

If your child is having trouble with multiplication facts, give short (five-minute) reviews at home, concentrating on the facts he or she finds difficult.

Another important focus in this unit is on reading and writing big numbers. Big numbers are part of our everyday lives. Students will use big numbers to solve problems and make reasonable estimates.

Sometimes it is helpful to write big numbers in an abbreviated form so that they are easier to work with. One way is to use **exponents**, which tell how many times a number is a factor. For example, 100,000 is equal to $10 * 10 * 10 * 10 * 10$. So 100,000 can be written as 10^5. The small raised 5 is called an exponent, and 10^5 is read as "10 to the fifth power." This will be most students' first experience with exponents, which will be studied in depth during fifth and sixth grades. Help your child locate big numbers in newspapers and other sources and ask your child to read them to you. Or, you can read the numbers and have your child write them.

The class is well into the World Tour. Students are beginning to see how numerical information about a country helps them get a better understanding of the country—of its size, climate, location, and population distribution—and how these characteristics affect the way people live. The next stop on the World Tour will be Budapest, Hungary, the starting point for an exploration of European countries. Encourage your child to bring to school materials about Europe, such as articles in the travel section of your newspaper, magazine articles, and travel brochures.

Please keep this Family Letter for reference as your child works through Unit 5.

Use with Lesson 4.11.

Vocabulary

Important terms in Unit 5:

billion 1,000,000,000, or 10⁹; 1,000 million.

estimate A close, rather than exact, answer; an approximate answer to a computation; a number close to another number.

exponent *See exponential notation.*

exponential notation A way to show repeated multiplication by the same factor. For example, 2^3 is exponential notation for $2 * 2 * 2$. The small, raised 3, is the exponent. It tells how many times the number 2, called the *base*, is used as a *factor*.

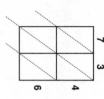

2^3 ← exponent
↑ base

extended multiplication fact A multiplication fact involving multiples of 10, 100, and so on. In an extended multiplication fact, each factor has only one digit that is not 0. For example, $400 * 6 = 2,400$ and $20 * 30 = 600$ are extended multiplication facts.

lattice multiplication A very old way to multiply multidigit numbers. The steps below show how to find the product $46 * 73$ using lattice multiplication.

Step 1: Write the factors on the outside of the lattice.

Step 2: Multiply each digit in one factor by each digit in the other factor.

Step 3: Add the numbers inside the lattice along each diagonal.

$46 * 73 = 3,358$

magnitude estimate A very rough estimate. A magnitude estimate tells whether an answer should be in the 1s, 10s, 100s, 1000s, and so on.

million 1,000,000, or 10⁶; 1,000 thousand.

partial-products method A way to multiply in which the value of each digit in one factor is multiplied by the value of each digit in the other factor. The final product is the sum of the several partial products.

Partial-Products Method

Multiply each part of one factor by each part of the other factor. Then add the partial products.

```
          73
        * 46
40 * 70 →  2800
40 * 3  →   120
6 * 70  →   420
6 * 3   → + 18
          3,358
```

power of 10 A whole number that can be written as a product using only 10s as factors. For example, 100 is equal to $10 * 10$, or 10^2; it is 10 to the second power.

rough estimate An estimate that is probably not very close to the exact answer. Rough estimates are often good enough for practical purposes.

round a number To replace a number with a nearby number that is easier to work with or better reflects the precision of the data. Often, numbers are rounded to the nearest multiple of 10, 100, 1,000, and so on. For example, 12,964 rounded to the nearest thousand is 13,000.

Do-Anytime Activities

To work with your child on concepts taught in this unit, try these interesting and rewarding activities:

1 To facilitate your child's ease in handling big numbers, have him or her look up the distances from Earth to some of the planets in the solar system, such as the distance from Earth to Mars, to Jupiter, to Saturn, and so on.

2 Have your child look up the box-office gross of one or more favorite movies.

3 Help your child look up the populations and land areas of the state and city in which you live and compare them with the populations and areas of other states and cities.

4 Have your child locate big numbers in newspapers and other sources and ask him or her to read them to you. Or, you can read the numbers and have your child write them.

Building Skills through Games

In Unit 5, your child will practice multiplication skills and build his or her understanding of multidigit numbers by playing the following games. For detailed instructions, see the *Student Reference Book.*

Multiplication Wrestling See *Student Reference Book* page 202.

This is a game for 2 players and requires 4 each of the number cards 0 through 9. The game reinforces understanding of the partial-products method for multiplication.

High-Number Toss See *Student Reference Book* page 201.

This is a game for 2 players and requires 1 six-sided die and paper and pencil. The game reinforces understanding of place value.

Number Top-It See *Student Reference Book* page 204.

This is a game for 2 to 5 players and requires a place-value mat and 4 each of the number cards 0 through 9. The game strengthens understanding of place value.

As You Help Your Child with Homework

As your child brings assignments home, you may want to go over the instructions together, clarifying them as necessary. The answers listed below will guide you through some of the Study Links in this unit.

Study Link 5.1

1. 1,104
2. 1,200
3. 832
4. 3,008
5. 1,854
6. 6,450

Study Link 5.2

Mike:

(50) * (20) = 1,000
(50) * (6) = 300
(2) * (20) = 40
(2) * (6) = 12
Score: 1,352

Jenny:

19 * 68 = (10 + 9) *
(60 + 8)
(10) * (60) = 600
(10) * (8) = 80
(9) * (60) = 540
(9) * (8) = 72
Score: 1,292

Kara:

38 * 32 = (30 + 8) *
(30 + 2)
(30) * (30) = 900
(30) * (2) = 60
(8) * (30) = 240
(8) * (2) = 16
Score: 1,216

Larry:

13 * 99 = (10 + 3) *
(90 * 9)
(10) * (90) = 900
(10) * (9) = 90
(3) * (90) = 270
(3) * (9) = 27
Score: 1,287

Study Link 5.3

Sample answers:

1. Estimate: 400 + 1,000 + 500 = 1,900; 1,824
2. Estimate: 400 + 700 = 1,100; 1,126
3. Estimate: 600 + 600 + 400 = 1,600; 1,595
4. Estimate: 800 + 700 = 1,500; 1,547
5. Estimate: 300 + 300 + 500 = 1,100; 1,107

Study Link 5.4

Sample answers:

1. Number model: 20 * 400 = 8,000; 1,000s
2. Number model: 10 * 20 = 200; 100s
3. Number model: 6,000 * 20 = 120,000; 100,000s
4. Number model: 10,000 * 50 = 500,000; 100,000s
5. Number model: 10 * 500,000 = 5,000,000; 1,000,000s

Study Link 5.5

1. **a.** 392
   b. 2,200
   c. 11,916
2. **a.** 36   **b.** 216
   c. 1,296   **d.** 1,554

Study Link 5.6

1. 1,680   2. 486
3. 3,266   4. 17,000
5. 4,074   6. 3,133

Study Link 5.7

7. 6,552

```
        7   8
   5¹ 6¹
  6  6   4  8
  5  8   2  4
  5  2
```

```
      84
    * 78
   5600
    280
    640
  +  32
   6552
```

Study Link 5.8

92,106,354,879

92 billion, 106 million, 354 thousand, 879

Study Link 5.10

1. 19,000; 24,000; 22,000; 18,000;
   19,000; 20,000; 20,000; 17,000
2. Boston Celtics and Milwaukee Bucks;
   New Jersey Nets and New York Knicks
3. 123,000,000; 151,000,000; 203,000,000;
   249,000,000

Partial-Sums Addition

Example $2,000 + 280 + 300 + 42 = ?$

$$
\begin{array}{r}
2000 \\
280 \\
300 \\
+\ 42 \\
\end{array}
$$

Add the thousands:	2000	
Add the hundreds:	500	$(200 + 300)$
Add the tens:	120	$(80 + 40)$
Add the ones:	2	
Find the total:	2622	

Solve each problem.

1. $800 + 120 + 160 + 24 =$ _____

2. $700 + 420 + 50 + 30 =$ _____

3. _____ $= 600 + 180 + 40 + 12$

4. _____ $= 2,400 + 160 + 420 + 28$

5. _____ $= 1,500 + 90 + 240 + 24$

6. $5,600 + 420 + 400 + 30 =$ _____

Multiplication Wrestling

SRB
202

Mike, Kara, Jenny, and Larry played a game of *Multiplication Wrestling*.

Who do you think got the highest score? _____

To check your estimate, fill in the blanks. Then find each player's score.

Were you correct? _____

Mike: 52 * 26

$$52 * 26 = (50 + 2) * (20 + 6)$$

(_____ * _____) = _____

(_____ * _____) = _____

(_____ * _____) = _____

(_____ * _____) = _____

Score: _____

Kara: 38 * 32

$$38 * 32 = (\_\_\_ + \_\_\_) * (\_\_\_ + \_\_\_)$$

(_____ * _____) = _____

(_____ * _____) = _____

(_____ * _____) = _____

(_____ * _____) = _____

Score: _____

Jenny: 19 * 68

$$19 * 68 = (\_\_\_ + \_\_\_) * (\_\_\_ + \_\_\_)$$

(_____ * _____) = _____

(_____ * _____) = _____

(_____ * _____) = _____

(_____ * _____) = _____

Score: _____

Larry: 13 * 99

$$13 * 99 = (\_\_\_ + \_\_\_) * (\_\_\_ + \_\_\_)$$

(_____ * _____) = _____

(_____ * _____) = _____

(_____ * _____) = _____

(_____ * _____) = _____

Score: _____

Use with Lesson 5.2.

SRB 155 156

Estimating Sums

For each problem, write a number model to estimate the sum.

- If the estimate is greater than or equal to 1,500, find the exact sum.

- If the estimate is less than 1,500, **do not** solve the problem.

Example 867 + 734 = _____

Estimate: $900 + 700 = 1,600$

$$
\begin{array}{r}
867 \\
+ 734 \\
\hline
1500 \\
90 \\
+ 11 \\
\hline
1601
\end{array}
$$

1. 374 + 962 + 488 = _____

Estimate: _____

2. 382 + 744 = _____

Estimate: _____

3. 581 + 648 + 366 = _____

Estimate: _____

4. 845 + 702 = _____

Estimate: _____

5. 318 + 296 + 493 = _____

Estimate: _____

Use with Lesson 5.3.

Estimating Products

Estimate whether the answer will be in the tens, hundreds, thousands, or more. Write a number model to show how you estimated. Then circle the box that shows your estimate.

1. A koala sleeps an average of 22 hours each day. About how many hours does a koala sleep in a year?

Number model _____

| 10s | 100s | 1,000s | 10,000s | 100,000s | 1,000,000s |

2. A prairie vole (a mouselike rodent) has an average of 9 babies per litter. If it has 17 litters in a season, how many babies are produced?

Number model _____

| 10s | 100s | 1,000s | 10,000s | 100,000s | 1,000,000s |

3. In the next three seconds, Americans will eat approximately 6,000 eggs. About how many eggs will they eat in the next minute?

Number model _____

| 10s | 100s | 1,000s | 10,000s | 100,000s | 1,000,000s |

4. In the next hour, French people will save 12,000 trees by recycling paper. About how many trees will they save in two days?

Number model _____

| 10s | 100s | 1,000s | 10,000s | 100,000s | 1,000,000s |

5. The average American consumes 11 pounds of chocolate each year. The population of Wyoming is about 500,000 people. About how many pounds of chocolate are consumed each year in Wyoming?

Number model _____

| 10s | 100s | 1,000s | 10,000s | 100,000s | 1,000,000s |

Multiplication

1. Solve the problems. Show your work in the grid below.

   a. 56 * 7 = _____   **b.** 8 * 275 = _____   **c.** _____ = 1,324 * 9

2. An old puzzle begins: "A man has 6 houses. In each house he keeps 6 cats. Each cat has 6 whiskers. And on each whisker sit 6 fleas."

   a. How many cats are there? _____

   b. How many whiskers are there on all the cats? _____

   c. How many fleas sit on all the cats' whiskers? _____

   d. Answer the last line of the puzzle: "Houses, cats, whiskers, fleas—how many are there in all?"

More Multiplication

Study Link
5.6

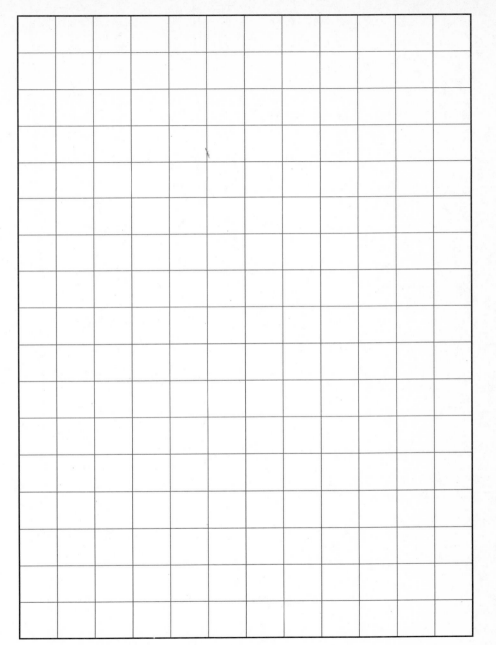

Multiply. Show your work in the grid below and on the back of this page.

Example 38 * 72 = ?

1,000s	100s	10s	1s
		7	2
		3	8
2	*	0	0	← 30 [70s]
	1	6	0	← 30 [2s]
	5	6	0	← 8 [70s]
		1	6	← 8 [2s]
+
2	7	3	6

1. 56 * 30 = _____

2. _____ = 27 * 18

3. _____ = 46 * 71

4. 340 * 50 = _____

5. 582 * 7 = _____

Challenge

6. _____ = 241 * 13

Use the lattice method to find the following products.

1. 5 * 46 = _____

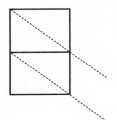

5

2. 8 * 67 = _____

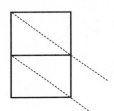

3. 7 * 836 = _____

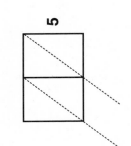

8 3 6 7

4. 4 * 329 = _____

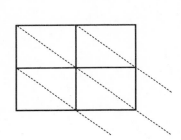

5. 25 * 31 = _____

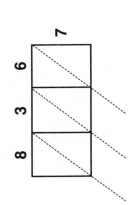

3 1 2 5

3
5

6. 49 * 52 = _____

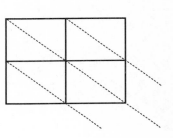

7. Use the lattice method and the partial-products method to find the product.

84 * 78 = _____

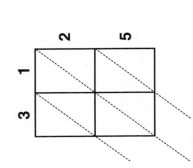

Place-Value Puzzle

Use the clues below to fill in the place-value chart.

Billions				Millions				Thousands				Ones		
100 B	10 B	1B	,	100M	10 M	1M	,	100Th	10Th	1Th	,	100	10	1
														1

Clues:

1. Find $\frac{1}{2}$ of 24. Subtract 4. Write the result in the hundreds place.

2. Find $\frac{1}{2}$ of 30. Divide the result by 3. Write the answer in the ten-thousands place.

3. Find $\frac{1}{10}$ of 30. Double the result and write it in the one-millions place.

4. Find $\frac{3}{4}$ of 12 and write it in the ones place.

5. Find 9 * 8. Reverse the digits in the result and divide by 9. Write the answer in the hundred-thousands place.

6. Double 8. Divide the result by 4. Write the answer in the one-thousands place.

7. In the one-billions place, write the even number greater than 0 that has not been used yet.

8. Write $\frac{5}{5}$ as a whole number in the hundred-millions place.

9. In the tens place, write the odd number that has not been used yet.

10. Find the sum of all the digits in the chart so far. Divide the result by 5 and write it in the ten-billions place.

11. Write 0 in the empty column whose place value is less than billions.

Write the number in words. For example, 17,450,206 would be written as "17 million, 450 thousand, 206."

_____

Estimating the Sizes of Numbers

For each item in the table below, estimate the size of the number and make an X in the appropriate column.

Example Most new cars cost at least $10,000. This means that the cost of a new car is in the ten-thousands.

Item	Hundred-Thousands	Ten-Thousands	Thousands	Hundreds	Tens	Ones
Cost of a new car (in dollars)		X				
Amount of food eaten by a person per day (in pounds)						
Distance from New York to Los Angeles (in miles)						
Distance around Earth at the equator (in miles)						
Speed of a car (in miles per hour)						
Speed of a jet plane (in miles per hour)						
Weight of an African elephant (in pounds)						
Height of the tallest tree in the world (in feet)						
Number of seats in a major-league baseball stadium						
Number of steps to the top of the Empire State Building, which has 102 floors						

Rounding

1. Round the seating capacities in the table to the nearest thousand.

National Basketball Association
Seating Capacity of Home Courts

Team	Seating Capacity	Seating Capacity Rounded to the Nearest 1,000
Boston Celtics	18,624	
Charlotte Hornets	24,042	
Chicago Bulls	21,711	
Indiana Pacers	18,400	
Milwaukee Bucks	18,717	
New Jersey Nets	20,049	
New York Knicks	19,763	
Seattle Supersonics	17,072	

Source: 1999 World Almanac

2. Look at your rounded numbers. Which teams' stadiums have about the same capacity?

_____

3. Round the population figures in the table to the nearest million.

U.S. Population by Official Census
from 1930 to 1990

Year	Population	Rounded to the Nearest Million
1930	123,202,624	
1950	151,325,798	
1970	203,302,031	
1990	248,718,301	

Source: The World Almanac and Book of Facts 1997

Use with Lesson 5.10.

113

Comparing Data

The table below shows the number of gallons of cow's milk produced by certain countries in 1997. Read each of these numbers aloud to a friend or a family member.

Country	Gallons of Milk
Brazil	4,898,768,000
France	6,406,870,400
Germany	7,373,800,000
India	8,848,560,000
Netherlands	2,869,498,240
Poland	2,923,872,000
Russia	8,720,320,000
Ukraine	3,924,144,000
United Kingdom	3,798,032,784
United States	18,228,546,560

1 gallon of milk contains
16 cups of milk.

1. Which country produced the most milk in 1997? _____

2. Which country produced the least amount of milk in 1997? _____

For each pair, circle the country that produced more milk.

3. Brazil   Germany

4. United States   France

5. India   Russia

6. Ukraine   United Kingdom

7. Netherlands   Poland

Unit 6: Division; Map Reference Frames; Measures of Angles

The first four lessons of Unit 6 focus on understanding the division operation, developing a method for dividing whole numbers, and solving division number stories.

Although most adults will reach for a calculator to do a long-division problem, it is useful to know a paper-and-pencil procedure for computations such as $567 \div 6$ and $15\overline{)235}$. Fortunately, there is a method that is similar to the one most of us learned in school but is much easier to understand and use. The method is presented in this unit.

Students have had considerable practice with extended division facts, such as $420 \div 7 = 60$, and questions such as "About how many 12s are in 150?" Using the "low stress" method called the partial-quotients method, your child will apply these skills to build up partial quotients until the exact quotient and remainder are determined.

The second focus in this unit is on numbers in map coordinate systems. For maps of relatively small areas, rectangular coordinate grids are used. For world maps and the world globe, the system of latitude and longitude is used to locate places.

Since this global system is based on angle measures, the class will practice measuring and drawing angles with circular (360°) and half-circle (180°) protractors. If you have a protractor, ask your child to show you how to use this tool.

The class is well into the World Tour. Students have visited Africa and are now traveling in Europe. They are beginning to see how numerical information about a country helps them get a better understanding of the country—its size, climate, location, and population distribution—and how these characteristics affect the way people live. Your child may want to share with you information about some of the countries the class has visited. Encourage your child to take materials about Europe to school, such as magazine articles, travel brochures, and articles in the travel section of your newspaper.

Circular (360°) protractor

Half-circle (180°) protractor

Please keep this Family Letter for reference as your child works through Unit 6.

Use with Lesson 5.12.

Vocabulary

Important terms in Unit 6:

acute angle An angle with a measure greater than 0° and less than 90°.

coordinate grid A device for locating points in a plane using *ordered number pairs*, or *coordinates*.

acute
angle

equal-groups notation A way to denote a number of equal-sized groups. The size of the groups is written inside square brackets and the number of groups is written in front of the brackets. For example, 3[6s] means 3 groups with 6 in each group.

index of locations A list of places together with a system for locating them on a map. For example, "Billings D3," indicates that Billings can be found within the rectangle where column 3 and row D meet on the map.

meridian bar A device on a globe that shows degrees of latitude north and south of the equator.

multiplication/division diagram A diagram used for problems in which there are several equal groups. The diagram has three parts: a number of groups, a number in each group, and a total number.

rows	chairs per row	chairs
6	4	24

obtuse angle An angle with a measure greater than 90° and less than 180°.

obtuse
angle

ordered number pair Two numbers that are used to locate a point on a *coordinate grid*. The first number gives the position along the horizontal axis, and the second number gives the position along the vertical

axis. The numbers in an ordered pair are called *coordinates*. Ordered pairs are usually written within parentheses: (2,3).

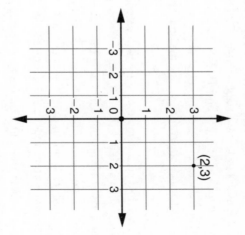

(2,3)

protractor A tool for measuring or drawing angles. A half-circle protractor can be used to measure and draw angles up to 180°; a full-circle protractor can be used to measure and draw angles up to 360°.

quotient The result of dividing one number by another number. For example, in 35 ÷ 5 = 7, the quotient is 7.

reflex angle An angle with a measure greater than 180° and less than 360°.

straight angle An angle with a measure of 180°.

vertex The point at which the rays of an angle, the sides of a polygon, or the edges of a polyhedron meet.

Family Letter, continued

To work with your child on concepts taught in this unit, try these interesting and rewarding activities:

1 Help your child practice division by solving problems for everyday situations.

2 Name places on the world globe and ask your child to give the latitude and longitude for each.

3 Encourage your child to identify and classify acute, right, obtuse, straight, and reflex angles in buildings, bridges, and other structures.

4 Work together with your child to construct a map, coordinate system, and index of locations for your neighborhood.

Building Skills through Games

In Unit 6, your child will practice using division and reference frames by playing the following games. For detailed instructions, see the *Student Reference Book.*

Division Dash *See Student Reference Book,* page 195.

This is a game for one or two players. Each player will need a calculator. The game helps students practice division and mental calculation.

Grid Search *See Student Reference Book,* pages 199 and 200.

This is a game for two players, and each player will require *two* playing grids. The game helps students practice using a letter-number coordinate system and developing a search strategy.

Robot

One player is the Controller, and the other is the Robot. The Controller picks a destination, giving the Robot directions for the amount of each turn and number of steps until the Robot reaches the destination. The amount of each turn may be given as a fraction of a full turn or as a degree measure.

Example: "Make a half turn and go forward 5 steps. Now turn clockwise 90 degrees and go back 3 steps."

As You Help Your Child with Homework

As your child brings assignments home, you may want to go over the instructions together, clarifying them as necessary. The answers listed below will guide you through some of this unit's Study Links.

Study Link 6.1

1. 38 6-packs
2. 38 tables
3. 37 R6
4. 47 R1
5. 23 teams
6. 72 bags

Study Link 6.2

1. 53 R3
2. 184 R3
3. 46 R10
4. Answer: 11 shelves
   Number model: $165 \div 15 = 11$

Study Link 6.3

1.

pages	cards per page	cards in all
?	6	744

Answer: 124 pages
Number model: $744 \div 6 = 124$

2.

porcupines	quills per porcupine	quills in all
4	30,000	?

Answer: About 120,000 quills
Number model: $4 * 30,000 = 120,000$

3.

boxes	calculators per box	calculators in all
?	14	364

Answer: 26 boxes
Number model: $364 \div 14 = 26$

Study Link 6.4

1. 21 sets
2. 9 shelves
3. 14 batches
4. 5 strawberries

Study Link 6.7

1. $90°; 180°; 270°; 360°$
2. a. Angle D
   b. Angle C
   c. Angle B
   d. Angle A

Study Link 6.8

1. $60°$
2. $150°$
3. $84°$
4. $105°$
5. $32°$
6. $300°$

Study Link 6.10

1. *B*
2. *C*
3. *D*

Study Link 6.6

Study Link 6.9

1.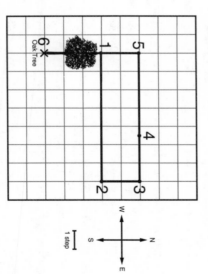

Study Link 6.11

1.
2. Eastern Hemisphere
3. water

Name _____ Date _____ Time _____

A Multiples-of-10 Strategy for Division

For Problems 1–4, fill in the multiples-of-10 list. Use the completed list to help answer the question. Write a number model.

1. The community center bought 228 cans of soda for the picnic. How many 6-packs is that?

10 [6s] = _____

20 [6s] = _____

30 [6s] = _____

40 [6s] = _____

50 [6s] = _____

Answer: _____ 6-packs

Number model: 228 ÷ 6 = _____

2. We have tables that each seat 5 people. How many tables are needed to seat 190 people?

10 [5s] = _____

20 [5s] = _____

30 [5s] = _____

40 [5s] = _____

50 [5s] = _____

Answer: _____ tables

Number model: _____ ÷ _____ = _____

3. How many 7s are in 265?

10 [7s] = _____

20 [7s] = _____

30 [7s] = _____

40 [7s] = _____

50 [7s] = _____

Answer: _____

Number model: 7)265

4. How many 3s are in 142?

10 [3s] = _____

20 [3s] = _____

30 [3s] = _____

40 [3s] = _____

50 [3s] = _____

Answer: _____

Number model: _____

5. There are 8 girls on each team in the basketball league. There are 184 girls in the league. How many teams are there?

Answer: _____ teams

Number model: 184 ÷ 8 = _____

6. José's class baked 290 cookies for the school bake sale. Students put 4 cookies in each bag. How many bags of 4 cookies did they make?

Answer: _____ bags

Number model: _____

Division

These notations for division are equivalent:

12)246   246 ÷ 12   246 / 12 $\frac{246}{12}$

Here is a method for dividing 246 by 9.

```
9)246         How many 9s in 246? At least 20.
−180    20    Use 20 as the first partial quotient. 20 * 9 = 180
  66          Subtract. At least 7 [9s] are left.
 −63    7     Use 7 as the second partial quotient. 7 * 9 = 63
   3    27    Subtract. Add the partial quotients. 20 + 7 = 27
   ↑    ↑
```

Remainder   Quotient   Answer: 27 R3

Now do these problems using this method—or one of your own.

1. 8)427   Answer: _____   **2.** 5)923   Answer: _____

3. 700 ÷ 15   Answer: _____

4. Adena has 165 stuffed bears. 15 bears
will fit on a shelf. How many shelves
does Adena need to display her bears?

Answer: _____ shelves

Number model: _____ ÷ _____ = _____

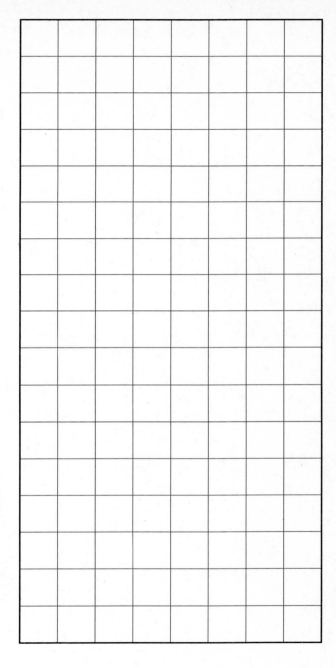

Multiplication and Division Stories

Fill in each Multiplication/Division Diagram. Then solve the problem and write a number model.

1. Trung's collection of 744 baseball cards is in an album. There are 6 cards on each page. How many pages of baseball cards are in the album?

pages	cards per page	cards in all

Answer: _____

Number model: _____

2. An average porcupine has about 30,000 quills. About how many quills would 4 porcupines have?

porcupines	quills per porcupine	quills in all

Answer: _____

Number model: _____

3. There are 364 calculators for the students at Madison School. A box holds 14 calculators. How many boxes are needed to hold all of the calculators?

boxes	calculators per box	calculators in all

Answer: _____

Number model: _____

Rewriting and Interpreting Remainders

SRB
153

Solve. For each problem, think carefully about what to do with the remainder.

1. Ms. Chew has a can of buttons. She asks Maurice to divide the buttons into sets of 16 buttons each. There are 348 buttons in the can. How many sets of 16 can Maurice make?

_____ sets

2. Emma has 75 CDs. Each shelf holds 9 CDs. How many shelves does she need to hold her entire collection?

_____ shelves

3. Jake wants to make at least 160 brownies for the bake sale. Each batch makes about 12 brownies. He plans to charge 35 cents per brownie. How many batches does he have to make?

at least _____ batches

4. Mrs. Zis brought a box of 125 strawberries to the party. She wants to divide the strawberries evenly among 24 people. How many whole strawberries does each person get?

_____ strawberries

Grid Art

SRB
124

Study Link
6.5

Plot the following points onto the grid below. After you plot each point, draw a line
segment to connect it to the last one you plotted. *Remember to use your straightedge!*

(10,2); (4,2); (2,7); (4,12); (7,13); (13,13); (15,8); (13,3); (10,2); (12,7); (10,12); (4,12)

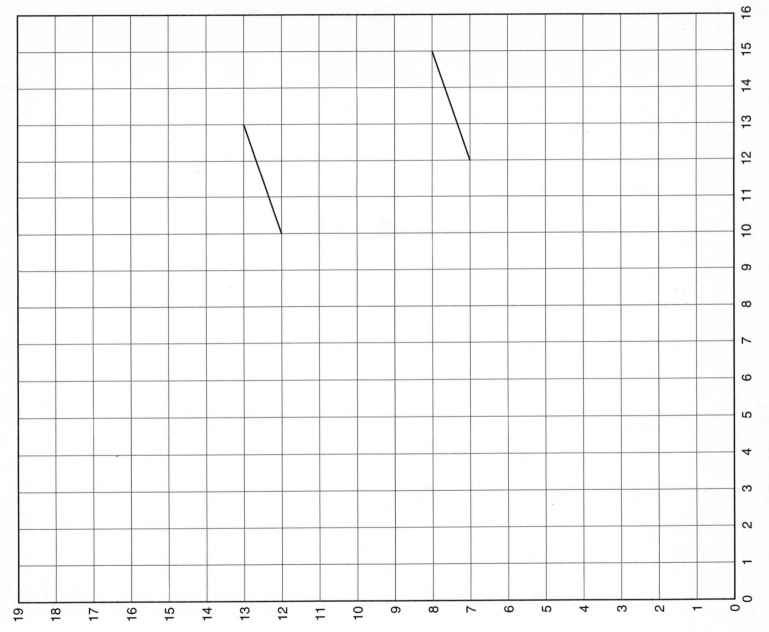

Nice work! You have just drawn a **hexagonal prism.**

Use with Lesson 6.5.

Treasure Hunt

Marge and her friends are playing Treasure Hunt. Help them find the treasure. Follow the directions. Draw the path from the oak tree to the treasure. Mark the spot where the treasure is buried.

1. Start at the dot under the oak tree; face north. Walk 3 steps.

2. Make a quarter turn, clockwise. Walk 7 steps.

3. Make a quarter turn, counterclockwise. Walk 2 steps.

4. Make a $\frac{3}{4}$ turn, clockwise. Walk $2\frac{1}{2}$ steps.

5. Make a full turn. Walk $4\frac{1}{2}$ steps.

6. Make a quarter turn, counterclockwise. Walk 5 steps.

7. Make an X to mark the spot where you end.

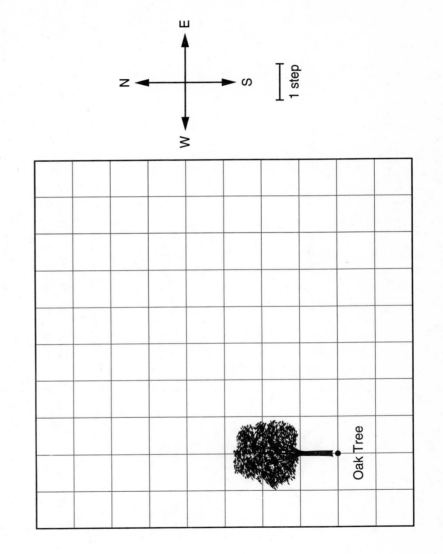

Oak Tree

Estimating Angle Measures

SRB
121 122

1. Complete the table.

Fill in the exact degree measure.

Rotation	Degree Measure
$\frac{1}{4}$ turn	
$\frac{1}{2}$ turn	
$\frac{3}{4}$ turn	
full turn	

2. Estimate which angle below shows a rotation

a. between 180° and 270°. Angle ____

b. between 0° and 90°. Angle ____

c. between 270° and 360°. Angle ____

d. between 90° and 180°. Angle ____

Use with Lesson 6.7.

133

Measuring Angles with a Protractor

Use a half-circle protractor. If you don't have one, cut out the protractor at the bottom of the page. Use a pencil to make a hole in the bottom of the protractor where the dot is.

Measure each angle as accurately as you can.

1. ∠A: _____°

2. ∠B: _____°

3. ∠C: _____°

4. ∠QRS: _____°

5. ∠NOP: _____°

6. ∠KLM: _____°

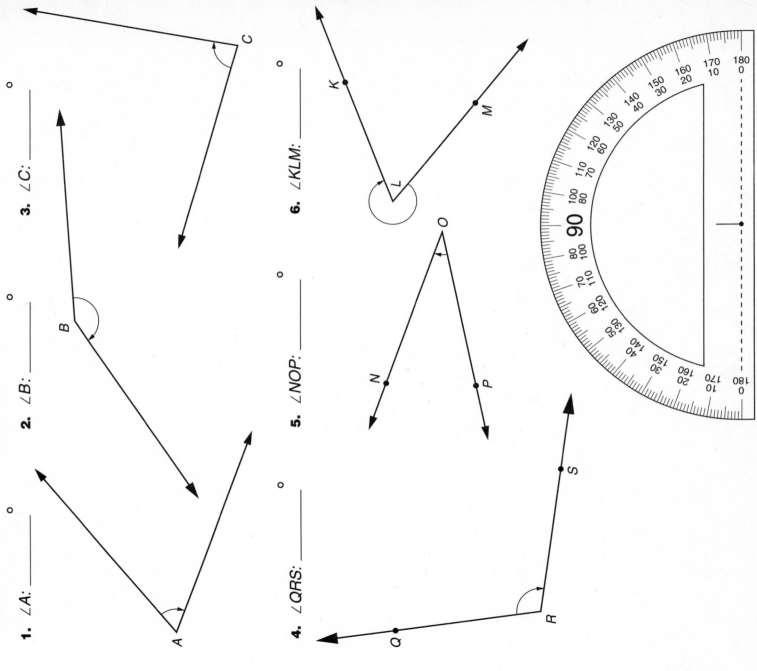

Use with Lesson 6.8.

135

The World Globe

You need your *Student Reference Book* to complete this Study Link.

Read pages 216 and 217. Read the examples and study the figures.

1. Do the following on the picture of the world globe.

   a. Draw and label the equator.

   b. Label the prime meridian.

   c. Label the North Pole.

   d. Label the South Pole.

   e. Draw a line of latitude that is north of the equator.

   f. Draw a line of longitude that is west of the prime meridian.

   g. Mark a point that is in the Southern Hemisphere and also in the Eastern Hemisphere. Label the point *A*.

   h. Mark a point that is in the Northern Hemisphere and also in the Western Hemisphere. Label the point *B*.

2. All of the continent of Africa is shown in the figure above. Is Africa mostly in the Western Hemisphere or in the Eastern Hemisphere?

   _____

3. Do the equator and prime meridian meet over water or over land?

   _____

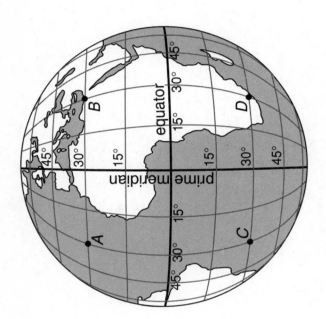

Find the following points on the picture of the globe. Write the letter of each point.

1. 30° North latitude and 30° East longitude _____

2. 30°S and 30°W _____

3. 30°S and 30°E _____

Mark the following points on the picture of the globe.

4. Point *E* at 15° South latitude and 45° East longitude

5. Point *F* at 45°N and 30°W

6. Point *G* at 30°N and 0°E

Family Letter

Unit 7: Fractions and Their Uses; Chance and Probability

In the unit just completed, your child practiced locating places on the globe using degrees of latitude and longitude with relation to the equator and the prime meridian. If you have a world globe or atlas, ask your child to show you how to use latitude and longitude to describe the locations of your hometown and other places of interest.

One of the most important ideas in mathematics is the concept that a number can be named in many different ways. For example, a store might advertise an item at $\frac{1}{2}$ off its original price or at a 50% discount—both mean the same thing. Much of the mathematics your child will learn involves finding equivalent names for numbers.

A few weeks ago, the class studied decimals as a way of naming numbers between whole numbers. Fractions serve the same purpose. After reviewing the meaning and uses of fractions, students will explore equivalent fractions—fractions that have the same value, such as $\frac{1}{2}$, $\frac{2}{4}$, $\frac{3}{6}$, and so on. As in past work with fractions, students will handle concrete objects and look at pictures, because they first need to "see" fractions in order to understand what fractions mean.

Fractions are also used to express the chance that an event will occur. For example, if we flip a coin, we say that it will land heads-up about $\frac{1}{2}$ of the time. The branch of mathematics that deals with chance events is called **probability.** Your child will begin to study probability by performing simple experiments.

Special!!!

$\frac{1}{2}$ Off

Men's Dress Shirts

(Sale ends Sunday)

A measuring cup showing fractional increments

Please keep this Family Letter for reference as your child works through Unit 7.

Use with Lesson 6.11.

Vocabulary

Important terms in Unit 7:

denominator The number below the line in a fraction. In a fraction where the whole is divided into equal parts, the denominator represents the number of equal parts into which the whole (or ONE or unit) is divided. In the fraction $\frac{a}{b}$, b is the denominator.

$$\frac{5}{9} \leftarrow \text{denominator} \qquad 5\,/\,9 \leftarrow \text{denominator}$$

equal chance or equally likely When each of the possible outcomes for some situation has the same chance of occurring, the outcomes are said to have an equal chance or to be equally likely. For example, in tossing a coin there is an equal chance of getting heads or tails. Heads and tails are equally likely outcomes.

equivalent fractions Fractions that have different denominators but name the same amount. For example, $\frac{1}{2}$ and $\frac{4}{8}$ are equivalent fractions.

fair (coin, die, or spinner) A device that is free from bias. Each side of a fair die or coin will come up about equally often. Each section of a fair spinner will come up in proportion to its area.

A die has six faces. If the die is fair, each face has the same chance of coming up.

fair game A game in which every player has the same chance of winning.

---

mixed number A number that is written using both a whole number and a fraction. For example, $2\frac{1}{4}$ is a mixed number equal to $2 + \frac{1}{4}$.

numerator The number above the line in a fraction. In a fraction where the whole is divided into a number of equal parts, the numerator represents the number of equal parts being considered. In the fraction $\frac{a}{b}$, a is the numerator.

$$\frac{5}{9} \leftarrow \text{numerator} \qquad 5\,/\,9 \leftarrow \text{numerator}$$

probability A number from 0 to 1 that tells the chance that an event will happen. The closer a probability is to 1, the more likely the event is to happen.

whole (or ONE or unit) The entire object, collection of objects, or quantity being considered; the ONE; the unit; 100%.

"whole" box A box in which students write the name of the whole (or ONE or unit).

Whole
24 pennies

Do-Anytime Activities

To work with your child on concepts taught in this unit, try these interesting and rewarding activities:

1 Have your child look for everyday uses of fractions in grocery items, clothing sizes, cookbooks, measuring cups and spoons, and statistics in newspapers and on television.

2 Encourage your child to express numbers, quantities, and measures, such as a quarter of an hour, a quart of orange juice, a dozen eggs, and a pint of milk.

3 While grocery shopping, help your child compare prices by looking at shelf labels or calculating unit prices. Help your child make decisions about the "better buy." If a calculator is available, have your child take it to the store.

4 Have your child look for everyday uses of probabilities in games, sports, and weather reports. Ask your child to make a list of events that could never happen, might happen, and are sure to happen.

Building Skills through Games

In this unit, your child will work on his or her understanding of numbers and fractions by playing the following games. For detailed instructions, see the *Student Reference Book.*

Name That Number See *Student Reference Book,* page 203.

This is a game for 2 or 3 players and requires a complete deck of number cards. The game helps students review operations with whole numbers.

Fraction Top-It See *Student Reference Book,* page 197.

This is a game for 2 to 4 players and requires one set of 32 Fraction Cards. The game develops skill in comparing fractions.

As You Help Your Child with Homework

As your child brings assignments home, you may want to go over the instructions together, clarifying them as necessary. The answers listed below will guide you through some of the Study Links in this unit.

Study Link 7.2

1. **a.** 15 nickels   **c.** $0.30
2. **a.** 4   **b.** 12   **c.** 8
4. 12   5. 7   6. 28
7. 10   8. 30   9. 10
10. 12   11. 12   12. $2\frac{1}{2}$

Study Link 7.3

3. 8 cans

Study Link 7.4

1. Less than $1.00
2. $3\frac{3}{4}$ inches
3. $\frac{1}{6}$
4. $2\frac{3}{8}$
5. Sample answers:

$$\frac{1}{4} + \frac{1}{4} + \frac{1}{4} + \frac{1}{4} = 1$$

$$\frac{1}{4} + \frac{1}{4} + \frac{1}{4} + \frac{1}{4} + \frac{1}{4} = 1$$

$$\frac{1}{4} + \frac{3}{12} + \frac{3}{6} = 1$$

$$\frac{2}{4} + \frac{3}{6} = 1$$

Study Link 7.5

1. $\frac{5}{12}$ 2. $\frac{1}{6}$ 3. $\frac{1}{4}$
4.   5.   6.
7. $\frac{3}{4}$ 8. $\frac{1}{4}$ 9. $\frac{1}{3}$
10. no; Sample answer: It took more than 1 hour to drive, because $\frac{1}{2} + \frac{1}{3}$ is 1 hour, and $\frac{3}{4}$ is larger than $\frac{1}{2}$; or $\frac{1}{2} + \frac{1}{4} = \frac{15}{12}$.

Study Link 7.6

1. C, F, I   2. B, D
3. E, H   4. A, G

Study Link 7.7

1. =   2. ≠   3. =
4. =   5. =   6. ≠
7. ≠   8. =   9. ≠
10. 8   11. 3   12. 10
13. 18   14. 12   15. 12
16. Sample answer: You could tell her that the Equivalent Fractions Rule states that you will get an equivalent fraction if you multiply by (not add) the same number in the numerator and denominator. Or you could draw a picture to show that $\frac{1}{4}$ is not equal to $\frac{3}{6}$.

Study Link 7.8

Sample answers:

1. $\frac{2}{10}, \frac{1}{5}, \frac{20}{100}$ 2. $\frac{6}{10}, \frac{3}{5}, \frac{60}{100}$ 3. =
3. $\frac{5}{10}, \frac{1}{2}, \frac{50}{100}$ 4. $\frac{3}{4}, \frac{30}{40}, \frac{75}{100}$

Sample answers:

5. 0.3   6. 0.63
7. 0.7   8. 0.4
9. 0.70; $\frac{70}{100}$ 10. 0.2; $\frac{2}{10}$

Study Link 7.9

1. >   2. <   3. =
4. =   5. <   6. >
7. Answers vary.   8. Answers vary.   9. $\frac{1}{4}, \frac{4}{10}, \frac{3}{7}, \frac{24}{50}$
10. $\frac{1}{50}, \frac{1}{20}, \frac{1}{5}, \frac{1}{3}, \frac{1}{2}$ 11. $\frac{4}{100}, \frac{4}{12}, \frac{4}{8}, \frac{4}{5}, \frac{4}{4}$ 12. $\frac{1}{12}, \frac{3}{12}, \frac{7}{12}, \frac{8}{12}, \frac{11}{12}$

Study Link 7.10

3. 28   4. 27   5. 8
6. 30   7. 10   8. 36

Fractions

SRB
42 50

1. Divide the circle into 6 equal parts.
Color $\frac{5}{6}$ of the circle.

Whole
circle

2. Divide the rectangle into 3 equal parts.
Shade $\frac{2}{3}$ of the rectangle.

Whole
rectangle

3. Divide each square into fourths.
Color $1\frac{3}{4}$ of the squares.

Whole
square

Fill in the missing numbers on the number lines.

4.

0       $\frac{7}{10}$ 1

5.

0    $\frac{1}{4}$ 1   2

"Fraction-of" Problems

1. a. Fill in the "whole" box.

Whole

b. Circle $\frac{2}{5}$ of the nickels.

c. How much money is that? _____

2. Theresa had 24 cookies. She gave $\frac{1}{6}$ to her sister and $\frac{3}{6}$ to her mother.

a. How many cookies did she give to her sister? _____ cookies

b. How many did she give to her mother? _____ cookies

c. How many did she have left? _____ cookies

Solve.

3. $\frac{1}{3}$ of 18 = _____

4. $\frac{2}{3}$ of 18 = _____

5. $\frac{1}{5}$ of 35 = _____

6. $\frac{4}{5}$ of 35 = _____

7. $\frac{1}{4}$ of 40 = _____

8. $\frac{3}{4}$ of 40 = _____

9. $\frac{5}{8}$ of 16 = _____

10. $\frac{4}{9}$ of 27 = _____

11. $\frac{3}{5}$ of 20 = _____

12. What is $\frac{1}{4}$ of 10? _____ Explain. _____

Dividing Squares

Use a straightedge and the dots below to help you divide each of the squares into equal parts.

Example Squares A, B, C, and D are each divided in half in a different way.

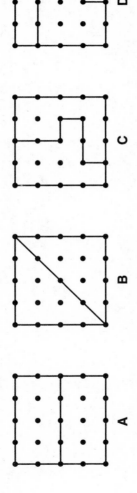

A   B   C   D

1. Square E is divided into fourths. Divide squares F, G, and H into fourths, each in a different way.

E   F   G   H

2. Square I is divided into eighths. Divide squares J, K, and L into eighths, each in a different way.

I   J   K   L

3. Rosa has 15 quarters and 10 nickels. She buys juice from a vending machine for herself and her friends. The juice costs 35 cents a can. She puts $\frac{2}{3}$ of the quarters and $\frac{3}{5}$ of the nickels in the machine and gets no change back.

How many cans of juice did she buy? _____ cans

Show your work on the back of this paper.

Use with Lesson 7.3.

Fractions

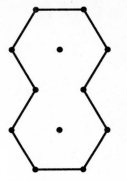

1. Jake has $\frac{3}{4}$ of a dollar. Maxwell has $\frac{1}{10}$ of a dollar.
   Do they have more or less than $1.00 in all? _____ inches

2. Jillian draws a line segment $2\frac{1}{4}$ inches long. Then she makes the
   line segment $1\frac{1}{2}$ inches longer. How long is the line segment now? _____

   $2\frac{1}{4}$ in. $1\frac{1}{2}$ in.

3. A pizza was cut into 6 slices. Benjamin ate $\frac{1}{3}$ of the
   pizza and Dana ate $\frac{1}{2}$. What fraction of the pizza was left? _____

   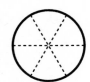

4. Rafael drew a line segment $2\frac{7}{8}$ inches long.
   Then he erased $\frac{1}{2}$ inch. How long is the line segment now? _____ inches

   $2\frac{7}{8}$ in.

   ? $\frac{1}{2}$ in.

5. Two hexagons together are one whole. Draw line segments to divide each
   whole into trapezoids, rhombuses, and triangles. Write a number model for
   each way you divided the whole.

   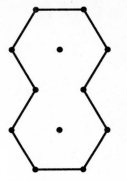

Use with Lesson 7.4.

Clock Fractions

Write the fraction represented by each clock face.

1.

_____

2.

_____

3.

_____

Shade each clock face to show the fraction. Start shading at the line segment.

4. $\frac{3}{4}$

5. $\frac{2}{3}$

6. $\frac{11}{12}$

Use the clock faces below to help you solve these problems.

7. $\frac{2}{3} + \frac{1}{12} =$ _____

8. $\frac{11}{12} - \frac{2}{3} =$ _____

9. $\frac{3}{4} - \frac{5}{12} =$ _____

10. It took Denise $\frac{3}{4}$ of an hour to drive from Zion to Platt, and $\frac{1}{2}$ hour to drive from Platt to Rome. To figure out her total driving time, Denise wrote the following number model: $\frac{3}{4} + \frac{1}{2} = \frac{4}{6}$

Do you agree that it took her about $\frac{4}{6}$ of an hour? _____

Explain. _____

Name _____ Date _____ Time _____

Many Names for Fractions

Write the letters of the pictures that represent each fraction.

1. $\frac{1}{2}$ ___C,_____

2. $\frac{3}{4}$ _____

3. $\frac{4}{5}$ _____

4. $\frac{2}{3}$ _____

A

B

C

D

E

F

G

H

I

Equivalent Fractions

For each pair of fractions below, ask yourself: "If I multiply both the numerator and denominator of one fraction by the same number, will I get the other fraction?"

- If the answer is *yes*, the fractions are equivalent. Write = in the blank.

- If the answer is *no*, the fractions are not equivalent. Write ≠ in the blank.
  (≠ means "not equal to")

1. $\dfrac{1}{3}$ —— $\dfrac{4}{12}$

2. $\dfrac{1}{4}$ —— $\dfrac{5}{12}$

3. $\dfrac{2}{3}$ —— $\dfrac{4}{6}$

4. $\dfrac{6}{8}$ —— $\dfrac{3}{4}$

5. $\dfrac{1}{2}$ —— $\dfrac{6}{12}$

6. $\dfrac{3}{6}$ —— $\dfrac{2}{3}$

7. $\dfrac{2}{5}$ —— $\dfrac{6}{10}$

8. $\dfrac{2}{3}$ —— $\dfrac{6}{9}$

9. $\dfrac{2}{6}$ —— $\dfrac{6}{12}$

In each box, write a number to make a fraction that is equivalent to the given fraction.

10. $\dfrac{4}{5} = \dfrac{\boxed{}}{10}$

11. $\dfrac{30}{40} = \dfrac{\boxed{}}{4}$

12. $\dfrac{15}{50} = \dfrac{3}{\boxed{}}$

13. $\dfrac{2}{3} = \dfrac{\boxed{}}{12}$

14. $\dfrac{8}{\boxed{}} = \dfrac{2}{3}$

15. $\dfrac{\boxed{}}{20} = \dfrac{3}{5}$

16. Margot says the value of a fraction doesn't change if you do the same thing to the numerator and denominator. Margot says that she added 2 to both the numerator and denominator in $\dfrac{1}{4}$ and got $\dfrac{3}{6}$.

Therefore, she says that $\dfrac{1}{4} = \dfrac{3}{6}$. How could you explain or show Margot that she is wrong?

$$\dfrac{1+2}{4+2} = \dfrac{3}{6}$$

_____

_____

_____

Fractions and Decimals

Write 3 equivalent fractions for each decimal.

Example

0.8 $\frac{8}{10}$ $\frac{4}{5}$ $\frac{80}{100}$

1. 0.20   _____   _____   _____

2. 0.6   _____   _____   _____

3. 0.50   _____   _____   _____

4. 0.75   _____   _____   _____

Write an equivalent decimal for each fraction.

5. $\frac{3}{10}$ _____

6. $\frac{63}{100}$ _____

7. $\frac{7}{10}$ _____

8. $\frac{2}{5}$ _____

9. Shade more than $\frac{53}{100}$ of the square and less than $\frac{8}{10}$ of the square. Write the value of the shaded part as a decimal and a fraction.

Decimal: _____

Fraction: _____

10. Shade more than $\frac{11}{100}$ of the square and less than $\frac{1}{4}$ of the square. Write the value of the shaded part as a decimal and a fraction.

Decimal: _____

Fraction: _____

Compare and Order Fractions

SRB
51 52

Write <, >, or = to make each number sentence true.

> < is less than
> > is greater than
> = is equal to

1. $\frac{5}{6}$ ___ $\frac{1}{6}$

2. $\frac{3}{10}$ ___ $\frac{3}{4}$

3. $\frac{2}{3}$ ___ $\frac{10}{15}$

4. $\frac{10}{40}$ ___ $\frac{4}{16}$

5. $\frac{4}{9}$ ___ $\frac{7}{9}$

6. $\frac{5}{6}$ ___ $\frac{5}{8}$

7. Explain how you solved Problem 1.

_____

_____

8. Explain how you solved Problem 2.

_____

_____

9. Circle each fraction that is less than $\frac{1}{2}$.

$\frac{7}{8}$ $\frac{1}{4}$ $\frac{4}{10}$ $\frac{7}{12}$ $\frac{5}{9}$ $\frac{3}{7}$ $\frac{24}{50}$ $\frac{67}{100}$

Write the fractions in order from smallest to largest.

10. $\frac{1}{5}$, $\frac{1}{3}$, $\frac{1}{20}$, $\frac{1}{2}$, $\frac{1}{50}$

___   ___   ___   ___   ___
smallest   largest

11. $\frac{4}{5}$, $\frac{4}{100}$, $\frac{4}{4}$, $\frac{4}{8}$, $\frac{4}{12}$

___   ___   ___   ___   ___
smallest   largest

12. $\frac{3}{12}$, $\frac{7}{12}$, $\frac{1}{12}$, $\frac{11}{12}$, $\frac{8}{12}$

___   ___   ___   ___   ___
smallest   largest

What Is the ONE?

For Problems 1 and 2, use your Geometry Template or sketch the shapes.

1. Suppose is $\frac{1}{4}$. Draw each of the following:

Example $\frac{3}{4}$

a. 1

b. $1\frac{1}{2}$

c. 2

2. Suppose 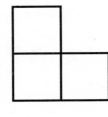 is $\frac{2}{3}$. Draw each of the following:

a. $\frac{1}{3}$

b. 1

c. $\frac{4}{3}$

d. 2

Solve.

3. If 14 counters are $\frac{1}{2}$, then what is the ONE? _____ counters

4. If 9 counters are $\frac{1}{3}$, then what is the ONE? _____ counters

5. If 6 counters are $\frac{3}{4}$, then what is the ONE? _____ counters

6. If 12 counters are $\frac{2}{5}$, then what is the ONE? _____ counters

7. If 8 counters are $\frac{4}{5}$, then what is the ONE? _____ counters

8. If 16 counters are $\frac{4}{9}$, then what is the ONE? _____ counters

Study Link
7.11

Spinners and Fractions

Design your own spinner. Use as many colors as you wish.

Describe your spinner. Tell the chance of the paper clip landing on each of the colors. Use sentences *like the following:*

- The chances of the paper clip landing on blue are 1 out of 3.

- The paper clip has a $\frac{3}{4}$ chance of landing on green.

- It is very unlikely to land on yellow.

- It is 3 times as likely to land on red as on blue.

- It has the same chance of landing on black as on white.

_____

_____

_____

_____

Layout of a Kitchen

Pages 167 and 168 will be needed to do Lesson 8.1 in the next unit. Please complete the pages and return them to class.

Every kitchen needs a stove, a sink, and a refrigerator. Notice how the stove, sink, and refrigerator are arranged in the kitchen below. The triangle shows the work path in the kitchen. Walking from the stove to the sink and to the refrigerator forms an invisible "triangle" on the floor.

Bird's-Eye View of Kitchen
(looking down at appliances and countertops)

The side of a square represents 1 foot.

Front View of Kitchen

1. Put one coin or other marker on the floor in front of your sink, one in front of your stove, and one in front of your refrigerator.

2. Measure the distance between each pair of markers. Use feet and inches and record your measurements below.

   Distance between

   a. stove and refrigerator   About _____ feet _____ inches

   b. refrigerator and sink   About _____ feet _____ inches

   c. sink and stove   About _____ feet _____ inches

Layout of a Kitchen (cont.)

3. On the grid below, make a sketch that shows how the stove, sink, and refrigerator are arranged in your kitchen.

Your sketch should show a bird's-eye view of these 3 appliances (including all countertops).

If your oven is separate from your stove, sketch the stove top only.

Use the following symbols in your sketch:

stove　　　　refrigerator　　　　sink　　　　double sink

Use with Lesson 7.11.

Chances Are ...

1. You are going to toss 2 pennies 20 times. Make a prediction.
   How many times do you think the 2 pennies will come up as

   a. 2 heads? _____ times

   b. 2 tails? _____ times

   c. 1 head and 1 tail? _____ times

2. Now toss 2 pennies together 20 times. Record the results in the table.

   A Penny Toss

Results	Number of Times
2 heads	
2 tails	
1 head and 1 tail	

3. What fraction of the tosses came up as

   a. 2 heads? _____

   b. 2 tails? _____

   c. 1 head and 1 tail? _____

4. Suppose you were to flip the coins 1,000 times.
   What fraction do you think would come up as

   a. 2 heads? _____

   b. 2 tails? _____

   c. 1 head and 1 tail? _____

5. Explain how you got your answers for Problem 4.

   _____

   _____

Family Letter

Unit 8: Perimeter and Area

In previous grades, your child studied the *perimeter* (distance around) and the *area* (amount of surface) of various geometric figures. This next unit will extend your child's understanding of geometry by developing and applying formulas for the areas of figures such as rectangles, parallelograms, and triangles.

Area of a Rectangle

Area = base * height (or length * width)

$A = b * h$ (or $l * w$)

Area of a Parallelogram

Area = base * height

$A = b * h$

Area of a Triangle

Area = $\frac{1}{2}$ of (base * height)

$A = \frac{1}{2} * b * h$

Students will learn how to make scale drawings and apply their knowledge of perimeter, area, and scale drawing by analyzing the arrangement of the appliances in their kitchens and the furniture in their bedrooms.

Students will also calculate the area of the skin that covers the entire body. A rule of thumb is that the area of a person's skin is about 100 times the area of one side of that person's hand. Ask your child to show you how to calculate the area of your own skin.

At the beginning of the year, the class learned to draw certain geometric figures using only a compass and straightedge. In this unit, your child will practice several new compass-and-straightedge constructions.

The World Tour will continue. Students will examine how geographical areas are measured, and difficulties in making accurate measurements. They will compare areas for South American countries by using division to calculate the ratio of areas.

Please keep this Family Letter for reference as your child works through Unit 8.

Use with Lesson 7.13.

Vocabulary

Important terms in Unit 8:

area The amount of surface inside a closed boundary. Area is measured in *square units*, such as square inches or square centimeters.

Area of a triangle

$A = \frac{1}{2} * b * h$

Area of a parallelogram

$A = b * h$

Area of a rectangle

$A = b * h$

formula A general rule for finding the value of something. A formula is often written using letters, called *variables*, that stand for the quantities involved.

length The measurement of something along its greatest dimension. The length of a rectangle is usually the longer dimension of the rectangle.

perimeter The distance around a closed 2-dimensional shape. The perimeter of a circle is called its *circumference*. The perimeter of a polygon is the sum of the lengths of its sides.

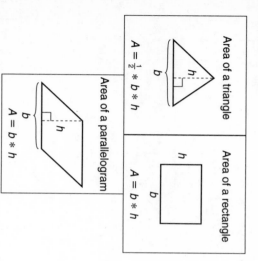

Perimeter of a rectangle

$p = l + w + l + w$
$= 2 * (l + w)$

perpendicular Meeting at right angles. Lines, line segments, and planes that meet at right angles are perpendicular. The symbol $\perp$ is read "is perpendicular to," as in "line $CD \perp$ line AB." The symbol $\llcorner$ indicates a right angle.

Perpendicular lines

scale The ratio of the distance on a map, globe, drawing, or model to an actual distance.

scale drawing A drawing of an object or region in which all parts are drawn to the same scale. Architects and builders often use scale drawings.

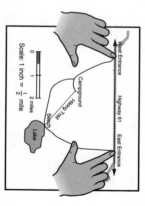

square unit A unit used in measuring area. For example, a square that measures one inch on each side has an area of one square inch.

variable A letter or other symbol that represents a number. A variable can represent one specific number or it can stand for many different numbers.

width The measurement of something along its shortest dimension. The width of a rectangle is usually the shorter dimension of the rectangle.

Do-Anytime Activities

To work with your child on concepts taught in this unit, try these interesting and rewarding activities:

1 Have your child pretend that he or she is a carpenter whose job is to redesign a room—for example, a bedroom, the kitchen, or the living room. Have him or her make a rough estimate of the area of the room. Then help your child check the estimate by finding the actual area using a tape measure or, if possible, blueprints.

2 Have your child pretend that he or she is an architect. Give him or her some dimensions and space requirements to work with. Then have your child design a "dream house," "dream bedroom," or sports stadium, and make a scale drawing for that design.

3 Work with your child to make a scale drawing of your neighborhood. Or have your child make a scale drawing of the floor plan of your house or apartment.

4 Have your child compare the areas of continents, countries, states, or major cities.

As You Help Your Child with Homework

As your child brings assignments home, you may want to go over the instructions together, clarifying them as necessary. The answers listed below will guide you through this unit's Study Links.

Study Link 8.1

1a. Perimeter = 19 feet 6 inches

1b. Perimeter = 20 feet 2 inches

2. Distance = 9 feet 3 inches; no

Study Link 8.2

1. a. 52

b. 117

c. $32\frac{1}{2}$

d. $175\frac{1}{2}$

3.

Rectangle	Height in Drawing	Actual Height
Rectangle A	$\frac{1}{2}$ in.	12 ft
Rectangle B	$1\frac{1}{4}$ in.	30 ft
Rectangle C	2 in.	48 ft
Rectangle D	$1\frac{3}{4}$ in.	42 ft
Rectangle E	1 in.	24 ft

Study Link 8.3

1. 24

2. 24

Study Link 8.4

1. 85,000

2. 17,500

Study Link 8.5

1. 78 ft

2. 27 ft

3. 2,106 sq ft

4. 2,808 sq ft

5. Sample answer: In a singles game, each player covers $\frac{1}{2}$ of 2,106 sq ft, or 1,053 sq ft. In a doubles game, each player covers $\frac{1}{4}$ of 2,808 sq ft, or 702 sq ft.

Study Link 8.6

1. 36

2. $29\frac{1}{4}$

3. 24

4. 46.8

5. 13

6. 8.5

Study Link 8.7

1. 16

2. 30

3. 12.75, or $12\frac{3}{4}$

4. 11.25, or $11\frac{1}{4}$

5. 3

6. 6

Study Link 8.8

1. Russia and Mexico and Brazil

2. Pakistan and Argentina

3. 5

4. 10, or 11

5. $\frac{1}{2}$

6. 9 or 10

Work Triangles

Recommended distances between appliances:

Between stove and refrigerator: 4 feet to 9 feet

Between refrigerator and sink: 4 feet to 7 feet

Between sink and stove: 4 feet to 6 feet

1. Find the perimeter of each of the work triangles below. Convert measures of 12 inches or more to feet and inches. (For example, 15 feet 16 inches = 16 feet 4 inches.) Circle the triangle whose sides are within the recommended range.

a.

sink   6' 3"   refrigerator

4' 8"   8' 7"

stove

Perimeter = _____ feet _____ inches

b.

refrigerator

8' 6"   7' 5"

stove

4' 3"   sink

Perimeter = _____ feet _____ inches

2. The perimeter of the work triangle below is 20 feet 6 inches.

a. What is the distance between the refrigerator and the sink?

_____ feet _____ inches

refrigerator   ?   sink

6' 6"   4' 9"

stove

b. Does this kitchen meet the recommendations? _____

Scale

SRB 125

1. If 1 inch on a map represents 13 miles, then

   a. 4 inches represent _____ miles.

   b. 9 inches represent _____ miles.

   c. $2\frac{1}{2}$ inches represent _____ miles.

   d. $13\frac{1}{2}$ inches represent _____ miles.

2. The scale for a drawing is 1 centimeter : 5 meters. Make a scale drawing of a rectangle that measures 20 meters by 15 meters.

3. Scale: $\frac{1}{4}$ inch represents 6 feet. Measure the height of each rectangle to the nearest $\frac{1}{4}$ inch. Complete the table.

A

B

C

D

E

Rectangle	Height in Drawing	Actual Height
A		
B		
C		
D		
E		

Exploring Area

1. Rectangle A at the right is drawn on a 1-centimeter grid. Find its area.

Area = _____ cm^2

A

2. Rectangle B has the same area as Rectangle A. Cut out Rectangle B. Then cut it into 5 pieces, any way you want.

Rearrange the pieces into a new shape that is not a rectangle. Then tape the pieces together in the space below. What is the area of the new shape?

Area of new shape = _____ cm^2

B

Areas of Irregular Figures

1. Here is a map of São Paulo State in Brazil. Each grid square represents 2,500 square miles. Estimate the area of São Paulo State.

   The area is about _____ square miles.

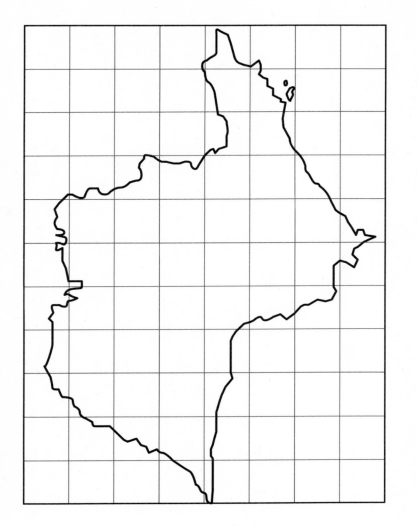

2. Here is a map of Rio de Janeiro State in Brazil. Each grid square represents 2,500 square miles. Estimate the area of Rio de Janeiro State.

   The area is about _____ square miles.

The Tennis Court

Area of rectangle = length * width

Tennis can be played either by 2 people or by 4 people. When 2 people play, it is called a game of singles. When 4 people play, it is called a game of doubles.

Here is a diagram of a tennis court. The net divides the court in half.

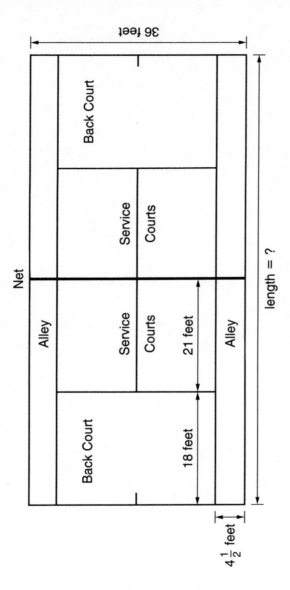

The two *alleys* are used only in doubles. They are never used in singles.

1. What is the total length of a tennis court? _____

2. The court used in a game of doubles is 36 feet wide. Each alley is
$4\frac{1}{2}$ feet wide. What is the width of the court used in a game of singles? _____

3. What is the **area** of a singles court? _____

4. What is the **area** of a doubles court? _____

5. Do you think a player needs to cover more court in a game of singles or in a game of doubles? Explain.

_____

_____

_____

Name _____ Date _____ Time _____

Areas of Parallelograms

Study Link
8.6

Find the area of each parallelogram.

1.

9'
4'

Area = _____ square feet

2.

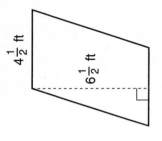

$4\frac{1}{2}$ ft
$6\frac{1}{2}$ ft

3.

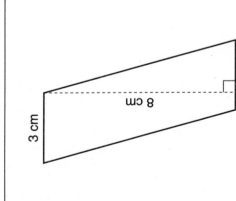

3 cm
8 cm

Area = _____ square centimeters

4.

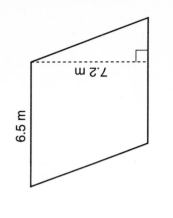

6.5 m
7.2 m

Area = _____ square meters

The area of each parallelogram is given. Find the length of the base.

5.

2 in.
?

Area = 26 square inches

base = _____ inches

6.

5.9 m
?

Area = 50.15 square meters

base = _____ meters

Use with Lesson 8.6.

185

Percents in My World

Percent means *per hundred* or *out of a hundred*. "1 percent" means $\frac{1}{100}$ or 0.01.

"48 percent of the students in our school are boys" means that out of every 100 students in the school, 48 are boys.

Percents are written in two ways: with the word *percent*, as in the sentence above, and with the symbol %.

Collect examples of percents. Look in newspapers, magazines, books, almanacs, and encyclopedias. Ask people at home to help. Write the examples below. Also tell where you found them. If an adult says you may, cut out examples and paste them on the back of this page.

Encyclopedia: 91% of the area of New Jersey is land, and 9% is covered by water.

Newspaper: 76 percent of the seniors in Southport High School say they plan to attend college next year.

Areas of Triangles

Find the area of each triangle.

1.

4'

8'

Area = _____ square feet

2.

5 cm

12 cm

Area = _____ square centimeters

3.

7.5 m

3.4 m

Area = _____ square meters

4.

$2\frac{1}{4}$ in.

10 in.

Area = _____ square inches

The area of each triangle is given. Find the length of the base.

5.

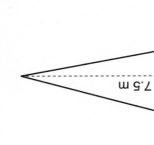

12 in.

?

Area = 18 square inches

base = _____ inches

6.

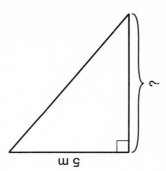

5 m

?

Area = 15 square meters

base = _____ meters

Daily Newspapers

Use the information in the table below to estimate the answers to the questions.

Country	Number of Daily Newspapers
India	1,802
United States	1,533
Germany	406
Turkey	400
Brazil	320
Mexico	310
Russia	292
Pakistan	223
Argentina	190
Greece	168

Source: The Top 10 of Everything 1999

1. India has about 6 times as many daily newspapers as which three countries?

 _____ , _____ and _____

2. Which two countries have about $\frac{1}{2}$ as many daily newspapers as Germany?

 _____ and _____

3. The United States has about _____ times as many daily newspapers as Mexico.

4. India has about _____ times as many daily newspapers as Greece.

5. Greece has about _____ as many daily newspapers as Brazil.

6. India has about _____ times as many daily newspapers as Argentina.

Family Letter

Unit 9: Percents

In Unit 9, we will be studying percents and their uses in everyday situations. Your child should begin finding examples of percents in newspapers and magazines, on food packages, on clothing labels, and so on, and bring them to class. Students' collections will be used to illustrate a variety of percent applications.

As we study percents, your child will learn equivalent values for percents, fractions, and decimals. For example, 50% is equivalent to the fraction $\frac{1}{2}$ and to the decimal 0.5. The class will develop the understanding that **percent** always refers to a **part out of 100.**

Converting "easy" fractions, such as $\frac{1}{2}$, $\frac{1}{3}$, $\frac{1}{10}$, and $\frac{3}{4}$, to decimal and percent equivalents should become automatic for your child. Such fractions are common in percent situations and are helpful with "more difficult" fractions, decimals, and percents. To aid in memorizing the "easy" fraction/percent equivalencies, your child will play Fraction/Percent Concentration.

"Easy" Fractions	Decimals	Percents
$\frac{1}{2}$	0.50	50%
$\frac{1}{4}$	0.25	25%
$\frac{3}{4}$	0.75	75%
$\frac{2}{5}$	0.40	40%
$\frac{7}{10}$	0.70	70%
$\frac{2}{2}$	1.00	100%

Throughout the unit, your child will use a calculator to convert fractions to percents and will learn how to use the percent key $\boxed{\%}$ to calculate discounts, sale prices, and percents of discount.

As part of the World Tour, your child will explore population data, such as literacy rates and percents of people who live in rural and urban areas.

Finally, the class will begin to apply the multiplication and division algorithms to problems that contain decimals. The approach used in Everyday Mathematics is quite simple: Students solve the problems as if the numbers were whole numbers. Then they estimate the answers to help them locate the decimal point in the exact answer. In this unit, we begin with fairly simple problems. Your child will solve progressively more difficult problems in Fifth and Sixth Grade Everyday Mathematics.

Please keep this Family Letter for reference as your child works through Unit 9.

Use with Lesson 8.9.

Vocabulary

Important terms in Unit 9:

discount The amount by which the regular price of an item is reduced.

life expectancy The average number of years a person may be expected to live.

literate and illiterate A literate person can read and write; an illiterate person cannot read and write.

100% box The entire object, the entire collection of objects, or the entire quantity being considered.

100% box

24 books

"24 books = 100%, the Whole, the ONE"

percent (%) Per hundred or out of a hundred. 1% equals $\frac{1}{100}$ or 0.01. For example, "48% of the students in the school are boys" means that 48 out of 100 students in the school are boys.

percent of literacy The percent of the total population that is literate; the number of people out of 100 who are able to read and write. For example, 90% of the population in Mexico is literate—this means that 90 out of 100 people can read and write.

percent or fraction discount The percent or fraction of the regular price that you save. See example under *regular price*.

rank To put in order by size; to sort from smallest to largest or vice versa.

Countries Ranked from Smallest to Largest Percent of Population, Ages 0–14	
1. Japan	15%
2. Russia	19%
3. Australia	21%
4. Thailand	24%
5. China	26%
6. Turkey	30%
7. Vietnam	33%
8. India	34%
9. Iran	36%
10. Bangladesh	38%

regular price or list price The price of an item without a discount.

Regular Price	Sale!	Sale Price	You Saved
$19.95	25% OFF	$14.96	$4.99

rural Living in the country.

sale price The amount you pay after subtracting the discount from the regular price. See example under *regular price*.

urban Living in the city.

Family Letter, *continued*

Do-Anytime Activities

To work with your child on the concepts taught in this unit, try these interesting and rewarding activities:

1 Help your child compile a percent portfolio that includes examples of the many ways percents are used in everyday life.

2 Encourage your child to incorporate such terms as "whole," "halves," "thirds," and "fourths" into his or her everyday vocabulary.

3 Practice renaming fractions as percents, and vice versa, in everyday situations. For example, when preparing a meal, quiz your child on what percent $\frac{3}{4}$ of a cup would be.

4 Look through advertisements of sales and discounts. If the original price of an item and the percent of discount are given, have your child calculate the amount of discount and the sale price. If the original price and sale price are given, have your child calculate the amount and percent of discount.

Building Skills through Games

In this unit, your child will work on matching fractions to equivalent percents, and vice versa, by playing the following game:

Fraction/Percent Concentration See *Student Reference Book,* page 196.

Two or three players need 1 set of Fraction/Percent Tiles and a calculator to play this game. Playing *Fraction/Percent Concentration* helps students recognize fractions and percents that are equivalent.

As You Help Your Child with Homework

As your child brings assignments home, you may want to go over the instructions together, clarifying them as necessary. The answers listed below will guide you through this unit's Study Links.

Study Link 9.1

1. $\frac{53}{100}$; 53%
2. $\frac{4}{100}$; 4%
3. $\frac{90}{100}$; 90%
4. $\frac{25}{100}$; 0.25
5. $\frac{7}{100}$; 0.07
6. $\frac{60}{100}$; 0.60
7. 0.75; 75%
8. 0.06; 6%
9. 0.50; 50%

Study Link 9.2

1. 100; $\frac{1}{100}$; 0.01; 1%
2. 20; $\frac{1}{20}$; 0.05; 5%
3. 10; $\frac{1}{10}$; 0.10; 10%
4. 4; $\frac{1}{4}$; 0.25; 25%
5. 2; $\frac{1}{2}$; 0.50; 50%
6. 0.75; 75%
7. 0.20; 20%

Study Link 9.3

1.

$\frac{1}{2}$	0	.	5				
$\frac{1}{3}$	0	.	3	3	3	3	3
$\frac{1}{4}$	0	.	2	5			
$\frac{1}{5}$	0	.	2				
$\frac{1}{6}$	0	.	1	6	6	6	6
$\frac{1}{7}$	0	.	1	4	2	8	5
$\frac{1}{8}$	0	.	1	2	5		
$\frac{1}{9}$	0	.	1	1	1	1	1
$\frac{1}{10}$	0	.	1				
$\frac{1}{11}$	0	.	0	9	0	9	0
$\frac{1}{12}$	0	.	0	8	3	3	3
$\frac{1}{13}$	0	.	0	7	6	9	2
$\frac{1}{14}$	0	.	0	7	1	4	2
$\frac{1}{15}$	0	.	0	6	6	6	6
$\frac{1}{16}$	0	.	0	6	2	5	
$\frac{1}{17}$	0	.	0	5	8	8	2
$\frac{1}{18}$	0	.	0	5	5	5	5
$\frac{1}{19}$	0	.	0	5	2	6	3
$\frac{1}{20}$	0	.	0	5			
$\frac{1}{21}$	0	.	0	4	7	6	1
$\frac{1}{22}$	0	.	0	4	5	4	5
$\frac{1}{23}$	0	.	0	4	3	4	7
$\frac{1}{24}$	0	.	0	4	1	6	6
$\frac{1}{25}$	0	.	0	4			

Study Link 9.4

1. 34%
2. 67%
3. 84%
4. 52%
5. 85%
6. 20%
7. 25%
8. 30%
9. 62.5%
10. 70%
11. 15%
12. 37.5%
13. Sample answer: I divided the numerator by the denominator and then multiplied by 100.
14. 86%
15. 3%
16. 14%
17. 83.5%

Study Link 9.5

1. 7%; 6%; 7%; 10%; 10%; 10%; 10%; 7%; 8%
2. Sample answer: I divided the first three digits of the number by 2,342 and multiplied the answer by 100. Then I rounded to the nearest percent.
3. No; Sample answer: Because each percentage was rounded to the nearest whole percent

Study Link 9.6

2. #2: 11; $\frac{5}{11}$; 45%
   #3: 3; $\frac{3}{3}$; 100%
   #4: 11; $\frac{9}{11}$; 82%
   #5: 7; $\frac{4}{7}$; 57%
   #6: 16; $\frac{11}{16}$; 69%
   #7: 10; $\frac{6}{10}$; 60%
   #8: 2; $\frac{1}{2}$; 50%
3. Sample answer: I would choose player #4, who has taken 11 shots and made 82% of her shots. Player #3 has a higher percent of shots made (100%), but she has taken only 3 shots.

Study Link 9.7

1. 54,000
2. 64,140
3. $\frac{1}{3}$
4. 50%
5. 64,000
6. 152,000
7. 17%

Study Link 9.8

1. 25.8
2. 489.6
3. 45.12
4. 112.64
5. 82878.6
6. 5.6
7. Sample answer: I estimated that the answer should be about 5 * 20 = 100.
8. 212.4
9. 38.64
10. 382.13

Study Link 9.9

1. 14.8
2. .2700
3. 24.96
4. .860
5. 23.4
6. 58.32
7. Sample answer: I estimated that the answer should be about 100 / 4 = 25.
8. 4.2
9. 38.7
10. 0.65

Fracions, Decimals, and Percents

Rename each decimal as a fraction and a percent.

1. $0.53 = \dfrac{\boxed{}}{100} = \underline{}\%$

2. $0.04 = \dfrac{\boxed{}}{100} = \underline{}\%$

3. $0.90 = \dfrac{\boxed{}}{100} = \underline{}\%$

Rename each percent as a fraction and a decimal.

4. $25\% = \dfrac{\boxed{}}{100} = \underline{}.\underline{}$

5. $7\% = \dfrac{\boxed{}}{100} = \underline{}.\underline{}$

6. $60\% = \dfrac{\boxed{}}{100} = \underline{}.\underline{}$

Rename each fraction as a decimal and a percent.

7. $\dfrac{75}{100} = \underline{}.\underline{} = \underline{}\%$

8. $\dfrac{6}{100} = \underline{}.\underline{} = \underline{}\%$

9. $\dfrac{50}{100} = \underline{}.\underline{} = \underline{}\%$

10. Shade more than 25% and less than 60% of the square.
Write the value of the shaded part as a decimal and a fraction.

Decimal: _____

Fraction: $\dfrac{\boxed{}}{100}$

11. Shade more than $\dfrac{10}{100}$ and less than $\dfrac{30}{100}$ of the square.
Write the value of the shaded part as a decimal and a percent.

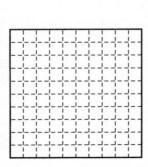

Decimal: _____

Percent: _____

12. Shade more than 0.65 and less than 0.85 of the square.
Write the value of the shaded part as a fraction and a percent.

Fraction: $\dfrac{\boxed{}}{100}$

Percent: _____

Trivia Survey

Conduct the survey below. The results won't be needed until Lesson 9.6.

Ask at least 5 people the following questions. You can ask family members, relatives, neighbors, and friends. You can ask the questions in person or by telephone.

Record each answer with a tally mark in the "Yes" or "No" column.

BE CAREFUL! You will not ask everyone every question. Pay attention to the instructions that go with each question.

Question	Yes	No
1. Is Monday your favorite day? (Ask everyone younger than 20.)		
2. Have you gone to the movies in the last month? (Ask everyone older than 8.)		
3. Did you eat breakfast today? (Ask everyone over 25.)		
4. Do you keep a map in your car? (Ask everyone who owns a car.)		
5. Did you eat at a fast-food restaurant yesterday? (Ask everyone.)		
6. Did you read a book during the last month? (Ask everyone over 20.)		
7. Are you more than 1 meter tall? (Ask everyone over 20.)		
8. Do you like liver? (Ask everyone.)		

199

Coins as Percents of $1

1. How many pennies in $1? _____

   What fraction of $1 is 1 penny? _____

   Write the decimal that shows what part of $1 is 1 penny. _____

   What percent of $1 is 1 penny? _____ %

2. How many nickels in $1? _____   What fraction of $1 is 1 nickel? _____

   Write the decimal that shows what part of $1 is 1 nickel. _____

   What percent of $1 is 1 nickel? _____ %

3. How many dimes in $1? _____   What fraction of $1 is 1 dime? _____

   Write the decimal that shows what part of $1 is 1 dime. _____

   What percent of $1 is 1 dime? _____ %

4. How many quarters in $1? _____   What fraction of $1 is 1 quarter? _____

   Write the decimal that shows what part of $1 is 1 quarter. _____

   What percent of $1 is 1 quarter? _____ %

5. How many half-dollars in $1? _____   What fraction of $1 is 1 half-dollar? _____

   Write the decimal that shows what part of $1 is 1 half-dollar. _____

   What percent of $1 is 1 half-dollar? _____ %

6. Three quarters (75¢) is $\frac{3}{4}$ of $1.

   Write the decimal. _____

   What percent of $1 is 3 quarters? _____ %

7. Two dimes (20¢) is $\frac{2}{10}$ of $1.

   Write the decimal. _____

   What percent of $1 is 2 dimes? _____ %

Calculator Decimals

SRB
168 169

1. Use your calculator to rename each fraction below as a decimal.

$\frac{1}{2}$	0	.	5				
$\frac{1}{3}$	0	.	3	3	3	3	3
$\frac{1}{4}$							
$\frac{1}{5}$							
$\frac{1}{6}$							
$\frac{1}{7}$							
$\frac{1}{8}$							
$\frac{1}{9}$							
$\frac{1}{10}$							
$\frac{1}{11}$							
$\frac{1}{12}$							
$\frac{1}{13}$							

$\frac{1}{14}$							
$\frac{1}{15}$							
$\frac{1}{16}$							
$\frac{1}{17}$							
$\frac{1}{18}$							
$\frac{1}{19}$							
$\frac{1}{20}$							
$\frac{1}{21}$							
$\frac{1}{22}$							
$\frac{1}{23}$							
$\frac{1}{24}$							
$\frac{1}{25}$							

2. Make up some of your own.

$\frac{1}{73}$	0	.	0	1	3	6	9 8
$\frac{1}{}$							
$\frac{1}{}$							
$\frac{1}{}$							
$\frac{1}{}$							

$\frac{1}{}$						
$\frac{1}{}$						
$\frac{1}{}$						
$\frac{1}{}$						
$\frac{1}{}$						

Use with Lesson 9.3.

Fractions and Decimals to Percents

SRB
60
168 169

Do **not** use a calculator to convert these fractions to percents.
Show your work for Problems 3–6.

1. $\dfrac{34}{100}$ = _____ %

2. $\dfrac{67}{100}$ = _____ %

3. $\dfrac{42}{50}$ = _____ %

4. $\dfrac{13}{25}$ = _____ %

5. $\dfrac{17}{20}$ = _____ %

6. $\dfrac{25}{125}$ = _____ %

Use a calculator to convert these fractions to percents.

7. $\dfrac{23}{92}$ = _____ %

8. $\dfrac{12}{40}$ = _____ %

9. $\dfrac{20}{32}$ = _____ %

10. $\dfrac{49}{70}$ = _____ %

11. $\dfrac{60}{400}$ = _____ %

12. $\dfrac{21}{56}$ = _____ %

13. Describe how you used your calculator to convert the fractions
in Problems 7–12 to percents.

_____

_____

_____

Do **not** use a calculator to convert these decimals to percents.

14. 0.86 = _____ %

15. 0.03 = _____ %

16. 0.140 = _____ %

17. 0.835 = _____ %

Use with Lesson 9.4.

Renaming Fractions as Percents

In 1996, there were about 2,342,000 marriages in the United States.
The table below shows the approximate number of marriages each month.

1. Use a calculator to find the percent of the total number of marriages that
occurred each month. Round the answers to the nearest whole percent.

Month	Approximate Number of Marriages	Approximate Percent of Total Marriages
January	100,000	4%
February	155,000	
March	147,000	
April	172,000	
May	241,000	
June	242,000	
July	235,000	
August	239,000	
September	225,000	
October	231,000	
November	171,000	
December	184,000	

Source: The Top 10 of Everything 1999

2. Describe how you used your calculator to calculate the percent for each month.

_____

_____

3. Do the percents in the table add up to 100%? _____ Explain why or why not.

_____

Use with Lesson 9.5.

Using Percents to Compare Fractions

1. The girls' varsity basketball team won 8 of the 10 games it played.
The junior varsity team won 6 of 8 games. Which team has the
better record? Explain your reasoning.

2. The record keeper for the varsity team kept a record of the shots taken by
each player (not including free throws) during the most recent game. Complete
the table. Calculate the percent of shots made to the nearest whole percent.

Player	Shots Made	Shots Missed	Total Shots	Shots Made / Total Shots	% of Shots Made
#1	5	12	17	$\frac{5}{17}$	29%
#2	5	6			
#3	3	0			
#4	9	2			
#5	4	3			
#6	11	5			
#7	6	4			
#8	1	1			

3. The basketball game is tied. Your team has the ball. There is only enough
time for one more shot. Based only on the information in the table, which
player would you choose to take the shot? Why?

Least Populated Countries

The table below shows the approximate population for the
10 least populated countries in the world.

Country	Approximate Population
Vatican City	860
Nauru	11,000
Tuvalu	11,000
San Marino	25,000
Monaco	32,000
Liechtenstein	32,000
Dominica	65,000
Marshall Islands	66,000
Seychelles	79,000
Kiribati	86,000

Use the data in the table to complete the statements.

1. There are about _____ more people living in Kiribati than Monaco.

2. The difference in population between Vatican City and Dominica

    is about _____ people.

3. The population of San Marino is about ⬜⬜ the population of Seychelles.

4. The combined population of Monaco and Liechtenstein is about _____ people.

5. The population of Liechtenstein is about _____ % of the population
    of Dominica.

6. The combined population of Kiribati and the Marshall Islands

    is about _____ people.

7. The population of Tuvalu is about _____ % of the population of the Marshall Islands.

Multiplying Decimals

Study Link
9.8

For each problem below, the multiplication has been done correctly, but the decimal point is missing in the answer. Correctly place the decimal point in the answer.

1. $6 * 4.3 = 2\ 5\ 8$

2. $72 * 6.8 = 4\ 8\ 9\ 6$

3. $0.96 * 47 = 4\ 5\ 1\ 2$

4. $5.12 * 22 = 1\ 1\ 2\ 6\ 4$

5. $8,457 * 9.8 = 8\ 2\ 8\ 7\ 8\ 6$

6. $0.04 * 140 = 5\ 6$

7. Explain how you decided where to place the decimal point in Problem 4.

_____

_____

Multiply. Show your work.

8. $5.9 * 36 =$ _____

9. $0.46 * 84 =$ _____

10. _____ $= 7.21 * 53$

Name   Date   Time

Dividing Decimals

For each problem below, the division has been done correctly, but the decimal point is missing in the answer. Correctly place the decimal point in the answer.

1. 88.8 / 6 = 1 4 8   **2.** 1.35 / 5 = 2 7 0 0

3. 99.84 / 4 = 2 4 9 6   **4.** 2.58 / 3 = 8 6 0

5. 163.8 / 7 = 2 3 4   **6.** 233.28 / 4 = 5 8 3 2

7. Explain how you decided where to place the decimal point in Problem 3.

_____

_____

Divide. Show your work.

8. 6)25.2   **9.** 4)154.8   **10.** 9)5.85

Answer: _____   Answer: _____   Answer: _____

Name

Date

Time

Family Letter

Study Link
9.10

Unit 10: Reflections and Symmetry

In this unit, your child will take another look at geometry, with an emphasis on symmetry. Many objects in nature are symmetric: flowers, insects, and the human body, to name just a few. Symmetry is all around—in buildings, furniture, clothing, paintings, and so on.

The class will focus on **reflectional symmetry,** also called **line symmetry** or **mirror symmetry,** in which half of a figure is the mirror image of the other half. Encourage your child to look for symmetric objects, and if possible, to collect pictures of symmetric objects from magazines and newspapers. For example, the right half of the printed letter T is the mirror image of the left half. If you have a small hand mirror, have your child check letters, numbers, and other objects to see whether they have line symmetry. The class will use a device called a **transparent mirror,** which is pictured below. Students will use it to see and trace the mirror image of an object.

Geometry is not only the study of figures (such as lines, rectangles, and circles), but also the study of transformations or "motions" of figures. These motions include **reflections** (flips), **rotations** (turns), and **translations** (slides). Your child will use these motions to create pictures like the ones below, called **frieze patterns.**

Students will also work with positive and negative numbers, looking at them as reflections of each other across zero on a number line. They will develop skills of adding positive and negative numbers by thinking in terms of credits and debits for a new company, and they will practice these skills in the *Credits/Debits Game.*

Please keep this Family Letter for reference as your child works through Unit 10.

Use with Lesson 9.10.

Vocabulary

Important words to keep in mind as your child works through Unit 5:

frieze pattern A geometric design in a long strip in which an element is repeated over and over. Frieze patterns are often found on the borders of rugs and tiled floors, and on clothing.

image A figure that is produced by a transformation of another figure. See *preimage* below.

preimage | line of reflection | image

line of reflection A line halfway between a figure (preimage) and its reflected image.

line of symmetry A line drawn through a figure that divides the figure into two parts that look exactly alike but are facing in opposite directions.

line of symmetry

negative number A number that is less than zero; a number to the left of zero on a horizontal number line or below zero on a vertical number line.

preimage A geometric figure that is somehow changed (by a *reflection*, a *rotation*, or a *translation*, for example) to produce another figure. See *image* above.

reflection (flip) The "flipping" of a figure over a line (the *line of reflection*) so that its image is the mirror image of the original (preimage).

reflection

rotation (turn) A movement of a figure around a fixed point or axis.

symmetry Having the same size and shape across a dividing line or around a point.

transformation An operation on a geometric figure that produces a new figure (the image) from the original figure (the preimage).

translation (slide) The motion of "sliding" an object or picture along a line segment.

translation

Family Letter, *continued*

Do-Anytime Activities

To work with your child on concepts taught in this unit, try these interesting and rewarding activities:

1 Have your child look for frieze patterns on buildings, rugs, floors, and clothing. If possible, have your child bring pictures to school or make sketches of friezes that he or she sees.

2 Encourage your child to study the mathematical qualities of the patterns of musical notes and rhythms. Composers of even the simplest of tunes use reflections and translations of notes and chords (groups of notes).

3 Encourage your child to incorporate transformation vocabulary—**symmetric, reflected, rotated,** and **translated**—into his or her everyday vocabulary.

Building Skills through Games

In this unit, your child will develop his or her understanding of addition and subtraction of positive and negative numbers by playing the following game. For detailed instructions, see the *Student Reference Book.*

Credits/Debits Game See *Student Reference Book,* page 192. Two players need 1 complete deck of number cards and a recording sheet to play this game. Playing the *Credits/Debits Game* offers students practice adding and subtracting positive and negative numbers.

As You Help Your Child with Homework

As your child brings home assignments, you may want to go over the instructions together, clarifying them as necessary. The answers listed below will guide you through some of the Study Links in this unit.

Study Link 10.2

1.

preimage | image

3.

preimage

image

5.

preimage

image

Study Link 10.3

1.

line of reflection

preimage

image

3.

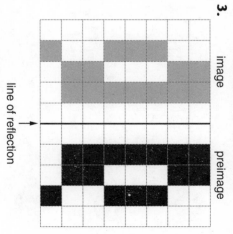

line of reflection

image

preimage

Study Link 10.4

2. A H I M O T U V W X Y

3. B C D E H I K O X

4. H I O X

5. O

6. Sample answers:

horizontal	vertical
BOX	TAX
KID	YOU
BOOK	MAT
KICK	HIM

Study Link 10.6

1. <   **2.** <

3. >   **4.** <

5. >   **6.** >

7. $-8, -3.4, -\frac{1}{4}, \frac{1}{2}, 1.7, 5$

8. $-43, -3, 0, \frac{14}{7}, 5, 22$

9. Sample answers: 0.3, 0.95, $\frac{8}{8}$, 1.99

10. Sample answers: $-2.4, -\frac{18}{9}, -1.67, -0.4$

11. 13   **12.** 2

13. -20 **14.** -2

15. 19   **16.** 7

17. -5 **18.** -22

Use with Lesson 9.10.

Family Letter, *continued*

Study Link 10.1

A Reflected Image

There is a simple design in the box in the middle of this page. It is the **preimage.**

Hold this page in front of a mirror, with the printed side facing the mirror. On a blank piece of paper, sketch what the design looks like in the mirror—the **image.**

Compare your sketch (image) with the design on the Study Link page (preimage). Bring both the preimage and image to school tomorrow.

mirror

back of Study Link

Sketch the design as it looks in the mirror.

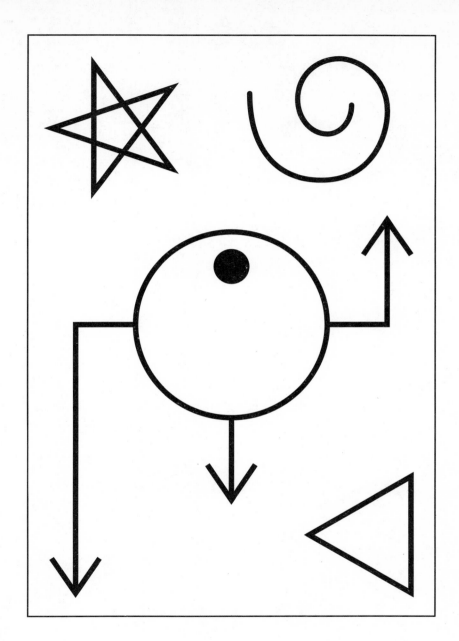

221

Use with Lesson 10.1.

Lines of Reflection

For each preimage and image, draw the line of reflection.

1.

preimage image

2.

image preimage

3. preimage

image

For each preimage, use your Geometry Template to draw the image on the other side of the line of reflection.

4.

preimage

5.

preimage

6.

preimage

Reflections

Study Link
10.3

SRB
92

Shade squares to create the reflected image of each preimage.

1.

preimage | image

line of
reflection

2.

preimage | image

line of
reflection

3.

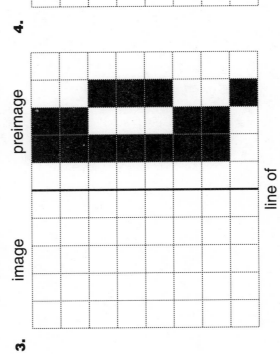

preimage

image

line of
reflection

4.

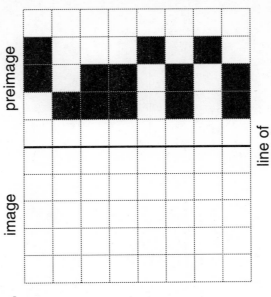

preimage

image

line of
reflection

Use with Lesson 10.3.

Line Symmetry in the Alphabet

1. Write the 26 CAPITAL letters of the alphabet below.

   _____

2. The capital letter A has a vertical line of symmetry.

   Name the other capital letters of the alphabet that have a vertical line of symmetry.

   A _____

3. The capital letter B has a horizontal line of symmetry.

   Name the other capital letters of the alphabet that have a horizontal line of symmetry.

   B _____

4. Which capital letters have both a vertical and a horizontal line of symmetry?
   (*Hint:* Find the letters that appear as answers in both Problem 2 and Problem 3.)

   _____

5. Which capital letter has an infinite (unlimited) number of lines of symmetry?

   _____

6. The word BED has a horizontal line of symmetry.   BED

   The word HIT has a vertical line of symmetry.   H I T

   Use capital letters to list words that have horizontal or vertical line symmetry.

   horizontal   **vertical**

   _____   _____

   _____   _____

   _____   _____

Use with Lesson 10.4.

227

Geometric Patterns

SRB
92–94

1. Continue each pattern. Then tell if you continued the pattern by using a reflection, rotation, or translation of the original design.

a.

b.

c.

2. Make up your own patterns.

a.

b.

Positive and Negative Numbers

Write < or > to make a true number sentence.

1. −7 _____ 7

2. 3 _____ 14

3. −8 _____ −10

4. 19 _____ 20

5. 8 _____ 0

6. 0 _____ −4

List the numbers in order from least to greatest.

7. 5, −8, $\frac{1}{2}$, −$\frac{1}{4}$, 1.7, −3.4

_____, _____, _____, _____, _____, _____
least   greatest

8. −43, 22, $\frac{14}{7}$, 5, −3, 0

_____, _____, _____, _____, _____, _____
least   greatest

9. Name four positive numbers less than 2.

_____ _____ _____ _____

10. Name four negative numbers greater than −3.

_____ _____ _____ _____

Add.

11. 4 + 9 = _____

12. 5 + (−3) = _____

13. _____ = −8 + (−12)

14. _____ = 7 + (−9)

15. 13 + 6 = _____

16. (−4) + 11 = _____

17. _____ = (−13) + 8

18. _____ = −9 + (−13)

Family Letter

Unit 11: 3-Dimensional Shapes, Weight, Volume, and Capacity

Our next unit introduces several new topics, as well as reviewing some of the work with geometric solids from previous grades and some of the main ideas your child has been studying this past year.

We begin with a lesson on weight, focusing on grams and ounces. Students handle and weigh a variety of objects, trying to develop "weight sense" so that they can estimate weights effectively.

As part of a review of the properties of 3-dimensional shapes (prisms, pyramids, cylinders, and cones), your child will construct models of geometric solids using straws and paper patterns. The class will also search for 3-dimensional objects that look like geometric shapes to put into a Shapes Museum. For example, someone might bring a can of soup to represent a cylinder. You might want to help your child find such objects.

By experimenting with cubes, the class will develop and apply a formula for finding the volumes of rectangular prisms (solids that look like boxes).

We will consider familiar units of capacity (cups, pints, quarts, gallons) and the relationships among them.

Your child will also explore subtraction of positive and negative numbers by playing a variation of the *Credits/Debits Game* introduced in Unit 10.

1 kg   1,000 g

In Lesson 11.1, a pan balance is used to measure weight in grams.

Please keep this Family Letter for reference as your child works through Unit 11.

Use with Lesson 10.7.

Vocabulary

Important words to keep in mind as your child works through Unit 5:

capacity The amount a container can hold. Also, the heaviest weight a scale can measure.

cone A 3-dimensional shape that has a circular *base*, a curved surface, and one vertex, which is called the *apex*. The points on the curved surface of a cone are on straight lines connecting the apex and the circumference of the base.

apex

base

apex

base

cubic unit A unit used in measuring volume, such as cubic centimeters or cubic feet.

curved surface A surface that is not flat.

cylinder A 3-dimensional shape that has two circular or elliptical bases that are parallel and congruent and are connected by a curved surface. The points on the curved surface of a cylinder are on straight lines connecting corresponding points on the bases. A can is shaped like a cylinder.

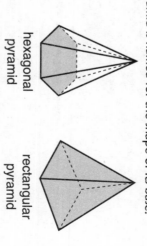

dimension A property of space; extension in a given direction. A straight line has one dimension, a square has two dimensions, and a rectangular prism has three dimensions.

formula A general rule for finding the value of something. A formula is often written using letters, called variables, that stand for the quantities involved. For example, the formula for the area of a rectangle may be written as $A = l * w$, where A represents the area of the rectangle, l represents its length, and w represents its width.

geometric solid A 3-dimensional shape, such as a prism, cylinder, cone, or sphere. Despite its name, a geometric solid is hollow; it does not contain the points in its interior.

---

pan balance A tool used to weigh objects or compare their weights.

prism A solid with two parallel *faces*, called *bases*, that are congruent polygons, and other *faces* that are all parallelograms. The points on the lateral faces of a prism are all on lines connecting corresponding points on the bases. A prism is named for the shape of its base.

triangular
prism

rectangular
prism

hexagonal
prism

pyramid A solid in which one face, the *base*, is any polygon and all the other *faces* are triangles that come together at a point called the *vertex* or *apex*. A pyramid is named for the shape of its base.

hexagonal
pyramid

rectangular
pyramid

3-dimensional (3-D) Solid objects that take up volume. 3-dimensional objects have length, width, and thickness.

volume The amount of space inside a 3-dimensional object. Volume is usually measured in cubic units, such as cubic centimeters or cubic inches. Sometimes volume is measured in units of capacity, such as gallons or liters.

weight A measure of the force of gravity on an object. Weight is measured in metric units such as grams, kilograms, and milligrams; and in U.S. customary units such as pounds and ounces.

Family Letter, *continued*

Do-Anytime Activities

To work with your child on the concepts taught in this unit, try these interesting and rewarding activities:

1 Have your child compile a list of the world's heaviest objects or things. For example, which animal has the heaviest baby? What is the world's heaviest man-made structure? What is the greatest amount of weight ever hoisted by a person?

2 Have your child compile a portfolio of 3-dimensional shapes. Images can be taken from newspapers, magazines, photographs, and so on.

3 Encourage your child to create his or her own mnemonics and/or sayings for converting between units of capacity and weight. One such example is the old English saying "A pint's a pound the world around." (1 pint = 16 oz = 1 lb)

Building Skills through Games

In this unit, your child will work on his or her understanding of operations with positive and negative numbers by playing the following games. For detailed instructions, see the *Student Reference Book.*

Credits/Debits Game *See Student Reference Book, page 192.*

This is a game for 2 players. Game materials include 1 complete deck of number cards and a recording sheet. The *Credits/Debits Game* helps students to practice addition of positive and negative integers.

Credits/Debits Game (Advanced Version) *See Student Reference Book, page 193.*

This game is similar to the *Credits/Debits Game* and helps students to practice both addition and subtraction of positive and negative integers.

As You Help Your Child with Homework

As your child brings home assignments, you may want to go over the instructions together, clarifying them as necessary. The answers listed below will guide you through this unit's Study Links.

Study Link 11.1

Answers vary.

Study Link 11.2

1. a. square pyramid   b. cone

   c. sphere   d. cylinder

   e. rectangular prism   f. triangular prism

2.

3. 6

Study Link 11.3

1. cone

2. square pyramid

3. hexagonal prism

4. octahedron

Study Link 11.4

Answers vary.

Study Link 11.5

1. a. 39 cm³   b. 30 cm³

2. a. 54 cm³   b. 97 cm³

3. a. 133 cubes   b. 137 cubes

Study Link 11.6

1. <   2. <

3. >   4. >

5. >   6. >

7. $-14, -2.5, -0.7, \frac{30}{6}, 5.6, 8$

8. $-7, -\frac{24}{6}, -\frac{3}{5}, 0.02, 0.46, 4$

9. Sample answers:

   $4 - 12 = -8$ $-20 - (-12) = -8$

10. Sample answers:

    $-50 + 20 = -30$ $-15 + (-15) = -30$

11. -110

12. -8

13. -8

14. 15

15. 14

16. -19

17. -70

18. 18

Study Link 11.7

Answers vary for Problems 1–4.

5. 4

6. 48

7. 2

8. 3

9. 3

10. 10

Weighing Objects

Study Link 11.1

Find a scale or balance around your house or borrow one from a neighbor.

Estimate the weight of 10 objects. Then use the scale or balance to weigh each object. This activity will help you improve your estimation skills.

Be sure to include units in all your estimates and measures.

Object	Estimated Weight	Measured Weight

Solids

1. The pictures below show objects that are shaped approximately like geometric solids. Identify each object as one of the following: **cylinder, cone, sphere, triangular prism, square pyramid,** or **rectangular prism.**

a.

Type: _____

b.

Type: _____

c.

Type: _____

d.

Type: _____

e.

Type: _____

f.

Type: _____

2. Mark Xs on the vertices of the rectangular prism.

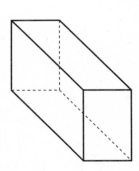

3. How many edges does the tetrahedron have? _____ edges

Geometry Riddles

Answer the following riddles.

1. I am a geometric solid.
I have two surfaces.
One of my surfaces is formed by a circle.
The other surface is curved.

What am I? _____

2. I am a geometric solid.
I have one square base.
I have four triangular faces.
Some Egyptian pharaohs were buried in tombs
shaped like me.

What am I? _____

3. I am a polyhedron.
I am a prism.
My two bases are hexagons.
My other faces are rectangles.

What am I? _____

4. I am a polyhedron.
All of my faces are the same.
All of my faces are equilateral triangles.
I have eight faces.

What am I? _____

Volume

Cut out the pattern below and tape it together to form an open box.

1. Find and record two items in your home that have volumes equal to
about $\frac{1}{2}$ of the volume of the open box.

_____

_____

2. Find and record two items in your home that have about the same volume
as the open box.

_____

_____

3. Find and record two items in your home that have volumes equal to
about 2 times the volume of the open box.

_____

_____

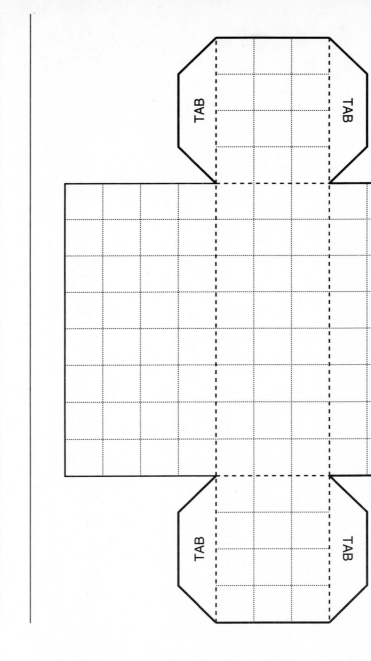

Name _____ Date _____ Time _____

Volume

1. Find the volume of each stack of centimeter cubes.

a.

Volume = _____ cm³

b.

Volume = _____ cm³

2. Calculate the volume.

a.

6 cm

3 cm

3 cm

Volume = _____ cm³

b.

2 cm

5 cm

9.7 cm

Volume = _____ cm³

3. How many more cubes are needed to completely fill each box?

a.

_____ more cubes

b.

_____ more cubes

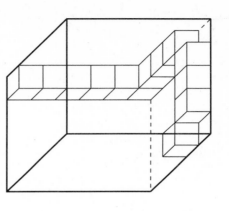

Positive and Negative Numbers

Write < or > to make a true number sentence.

1. 0 — 7 _____ −6

2. −11 _____ −13 − (−5)

3. 7 + (−2) _____ −8

4. 18 + (−8) _____ −18

5. 26 − (−14) _____ 27 + (−16)

6. 9 − (−11) _____ 0 + (−20)

List the numbers in order from least to greatest.

7. $\frac{30}{6}$, 8, −14, −0.7, 5.6, −2.5

_____ , _____ , _____ , _____ , _____ , _____
least   greatest

8. 0.02, $-\frac{3}{5}$, −7, 4, 0.46, $\frac{24}{6}$

_____ , _____ , _____ , _____ , _____ , _____
least   greatest

9. Write two subtraction problems with an answer of −8.

_____ − _____ = −8   _____ − _____ = −8

10. Write two addition problems with an answer of −30.

_____ + _____ = −30   _____ + _____ = −30

Add or subtract.

11. −40 + (−70) = _____

12. 12 − 20 = _____

13. _____ = −14 − (−6)

14. _____ = 10 − (−5)

15. 15 + (−1) = _____

16. −12 − 7 = _____

17. _____ = 60 + (−130)

18. _____ = −2 − (−20)

Name

Date

Time

Capacity

SRB
117

Container	Capacity Measurements on Label
bottle of hot chili sesame oil	5 fl oz, 148 mL

Container	Capacity Measurements on Label
bottle of cooking oil	16 fl oz, 473 mL

Container	Capacity Measurements on Label

Container	Capacity Measurements on Label

Unit 12: Rates

For the next two or three weeks, your child will be studying rates. Rates are among the most common applications of mathematics in daily life.

A rate is a comparison involving two different units. Familiar examples come from working (dollars per hour), driving (miles per hour), eating (calories per serving), reading (pages per day), and so on.

Our exploration of rates will begin with students collecting data on the rate at which their classmates blink their eyes. The class will try to answer the question, "Does a person's eye-blinking rate depend on what the person is doing?"

During this unit, students will collect many examples of rates to display in a Rates Museum. Then they will use these examples to make up rate problems, such as the following:

1. If cereal costs $2.98 per box, what will 4 boxes cost?

2. If a car's gas mileage is about 20 miles per gallon, how far can the car travel on a full tank of gas (16 gallons)?

3. If I make $6.25 per hour, how long must I work to earn enough to buy shoes that cost $35?

Then the class will work together to develop strategies for solving rate problems.

The unit emphasizes the importance of mathematics to smart consumers. Your child will learn about unit-pricing labels on supermarket shelves and how to use these labels to decide which of two items is the better buy. Your child will see that comparing prices is only *part* of being a smart consumer. Other factors to consider include quality, the need for the product, and, perhaps, the product's effect on the environment.

This unit provides a great opportunity for your child to help with the family shopping. Have your child help you decide whether the largest size is necessarily the best buy. Is an item on sale necessarily a better buy than a similar product that is not on sale?

Finally, students will look back on their experiences in the yearlong World Tour and share them with one another.

Nutrition Facts

Serving Size 1 link (45 g)
Servings per Container 10

Amount per Serving

Calories 150   Calories from Fat 120

	% Daily Value
Total Fat 13 g	20%
Total Carbohydrate 1 g	<1%
Protein 7 g	

Please keep this Family Letter for reference as your child works through Unit 12.

Use with Lesson 11.8.

Vocabulary

Important words to keep in mind as your child works through Unit 5:

comparison shopping Comparing prices and collecting other information needed to make good decisions about which of several competing products or services to buy.

consumer A person who acquires products or uses services.

per *In each or for each,* as in ten chairs per row or six tickets per family.

rate A comparison by division of two quantities with unlike units. For example, a speed such as 55 miles per hour is a rate that compares distance with time.

rate table A way of displaying *rate* information.

Rate Table

Miles	35	70	105	140	175	210
Gallons	1	2	3	4	5	6

unit price The price for one item or unit of measure. For example, if a 5-ounce package of something costs $2.50, then $0.50 per ounce is the unit price.

unit rate A rate with 1 in the denominator. For example, 600 calories per 3 servings $\left(\dfrac{600 \text{ calories}}{3 \text{ servings}}\right)$ is not a unit rate, but 200 calories per serving $\left(\dfrac{200 \text{ calories}}{1 \text{ serving}}\right)$ is a unit rate.

Do-Anytime Activities

To work with your child on concepts taught in this unit, try these interesting and rewarding activities:

1 Have your child examine the Nutrition Facts labels on various cans and packages of food. The label lists the number of servings in the container and the number of calories per serving. Have your child use this information to calculate the total number of calories in the full container or food. *For example:*

A can of soup has 2.5 servings.

There are 80 calories per serving.

So the full can has 2.5 * 80 = 200 calories.

2 Have your child point out rates in everyday situations. *For example:*

store price rates: cost per dozen, cost per 6-pack, cost per ounce

rent payments: dollars per month, or dollars per year

fuel efficiency: miles per gallon

wages: dollars per hour

sleep: hours per night

telephone rates: cents per minute

copy machine rates: copies per minute

3 Use supermarket visits to compare prices for different brands of an item, and for different sizes of the same item. Have your child calculate unit prices and discuss best buys.

Building Skills through Games

In this unit, your child will extend his or her understanding of addition and subtraction of positive and negative numbers by playing the following game. For detailed instructions, see the *Student Reference Book,* page 193.

Credits/Debits Game (Advanced Version) This game for 2 players simulates bookkeeping for a small business. A deck of number cards represents "credits" and "debits." Transactions are entered by the players on recording sheets that are easily drawn. The game offers practice in addition and subtraction of positive and negative integers.

As You Help Your Child with Homework

As your child brings assignments home, you may want to go over the instructions together, clarifying them as necessary. The answers listed below will guide you through this unit's Study Links.

Study Link 12.1

Answers vary.

Study Link 12.2

1. $315
2. $12
3. 14 hours

4. a. 364   b. 156

Minutes	52	104	156	208	260	312	364
Days	1	2	3	4	5	6	7

Hours	2	4	6	8	10	12	14
Days	1	2	3	4	5	6	7

Study Link 12.3

1.

Gallons	20	140	600	7,300
Days	1	7	30	365

7,300 gallons per year

2.

Gallons	300	2,100	9,000	109,500
Days	1	7	30	365

109,500 gallons per year

3.

Gallons	3	21	90	1,095
Days	1	7	30	365

90 gallons per month

4. 195,000 gallons

Study Link 12.4

Answers vary.

Study Link 12.5

1. $0.63
2. $0.37
3. $0.15
4. $0.15
5. $0.94
6. Sample answer: The 8-ounce cup costs $0.09 per ounce, and the 6-ounce cup costs $0.10 per ounce, so the 8-ounce cup is the better buy.

Study Link 12.6

1. 1,245
2. 9
3. a. 70
   b. 50
4. $\frac{1}{7}$
5. a. China
   b. Dem. Rep. of Congo, Germany, and Sudan
   c. 6
   d. $9\frac{1}{2}$
   e. 9

Examples of Rates

Look for examples of rates in newspapers, in magazines, and on labels.

Study the two examples below, and then list some of the examples you find.
If possible, bring your samples to class.

Example Label on a can of corn
says "Servings Per Container 3½"

Nutrition Facts
Serving Size 110 g
Servings Per Container 3 1/2
Amount Per Serving

Example Light bulbs come in cardboard holders that
have 4 bulbs. The holder doesn't say so, but there are
always 4 bulbs in each holder.

Example _____

_____

_____

_____

Example _____

_____

_____

Example _____

_____

_____

Rates

Solve the problems.

1. Hotels R Us charges $45 a night for a single room.
At that rate, how much does a single room cost *per week*?

$ _____

2. The Harrison family spends about $84 a week for
food. On average, how much do they spend *per day*?

$ _____

3. Sharon practices playing the piano the same amount
of time each day. She practiced a total of 4 hours
on Monday and Tuesday. At that rate, how many hours
would she practice *in a week*?

_____ hours

Hours							
Days	1	2	3	4	5	6	7

Challenge

4. People in the United States spend an average of 6 hours and 4 minutes
each week reading newspapers.

a. That's how many minutes *per week*?

_____ minutes per week

b. At that rate, how much time does an average
person spend reading newspapers in a *3-day period*?

_____ minutes

Minutes							
Days	1	2	3	4	5	6	7

Water Usage

According to the American Waterworks Association, Americans each use an average of 123 gallons of water a day for their personal needs. This seems like a large amount, but you may be surprised at how much water is used for even the shortest activities. For example, people use an average of 1 to 2 gallons of water just to brush their teeth. They use about 20 gallons of water when doing dishes by hand. They may use as much as 30 gallons when taking a shower.

For each problem, complete the rate table and answer the question.

1. If you use an average of 20 gallons of water when taking a shower and you take one shower a day, about how many gallons of water do you use in 1 year?

Gallons	20			
Days	1	7 (1 week)	30 (1 month)	365 (12 months)

Answer: About _____ gallons per year

2. The average American household uses about 2,100 gallons of water a week. About how many gallons of water does it use in 1 year?

Gallons	2,100			
Days	1	7 (1 week)	30 (1 month)	365 (12 months)

Answer: About _____ gallons per year

3. Madison uses about $1\frac{1}{2}$ gallons of water each time she brushes her teeth. She brushes her teeth twice a day. About how many gallons of water does she use in 1 month for brushing teeth?

Gallons	3			
Days	1	7 (1 week)	30 (1 month)	365 (12 months)

Answer: About _____ gallons per month

4. About 39,000 gallons of water are used in making 1 new car. About how many gallons of water are used to make 5 new cars? About _____ gallons

Supermarket Ads

Look in newspapers for supermarket ads. Choose some of the items in the ads.
Use the table below to record the price and quantity of each item.

Do not write anything in the Unit Price column.

Item	Quantity	Price	Unit Price
Golden Sun Raisins	24 ounces	$2.99	

Name _____   Date _____   Time _____

Unit Pricing

1. A package of 3 rolls of paper towels costs $1.89.
What is the price *per roll?* _____

2. A 5-pound bag of rice costs $1.85.
What is the price *per pound?* _____

3. Chewy worms are sold at $2.40 per pound.
What is the price *per ounce?* _____

4. A 6-pack of bagels costs 90 cents.
What is the price *per bagel?* _____

5. A 2-pound bag of frozen corn costs $1.88.
What is the price *per pound?* _____

6. A store sells yogurt in two sizes: the 8-ounce cup costs 72 cents, and the
6-ounce cup costs 60 cents. Which is the better buy? Explain your answer.

_____

_____

_____

7. Make up your own "better buy" problem. Then solve it.

_____

_____

_____

Name _____ Date _____ Time _____

Country Statistics

Study Link 12.6

SRB 149 150

1. China has the longest border in the world—13,759 miles. Russia has the second longest border in the world—12,514 miles. How much shorter is Russia's border than China's border? _____ miles

2. The area of Russia is about 1,818,629 square miles. The area of Spain, including offshore islands, is about 194,897 square miles. About how many times larger is Russia than Spain? About _____ times larger

3. Students in China attend school about 251 days per year. Students in the United States attend school about 180 days per year.

  a. About what percent of the year do Chinese students spend in school? About _____ %

  b. About what percent of the year do American students spend in school? About _____ %

4. English is officially spoken in 54 countries. Portuguese is officially spoken in 8 countries. Portuguese is spoken in about what fraction of the number of English-speaking countries? About _____

5. The table to the right shows the countries in the world with the most neighboring countries.

Country	Number of Neighbors
Brazil	10
China	15
Dem. Rep. of Congo	9
Germany	9
Russia	14
Sudan	9

Use the data in the table to answer the following questions.

  a. Which country has the maximum number of neighbors? _____

  b. Which countries have the minimum number of neighbors? _____

  _____

  c. What is the range? _____

  d. What is the median? _____

  e. What is the mode? _____

Use with Lesson 12.6.

265

Family Letter

Congratulations!

By completing *Fourth Grade Everyday Mathematics*, your child has accomplished a great deal. Thank you for all of your support.

This Family Letter is here for you to use as a resource throughout your child's vacation. It includes an extended list of Do-Anytime Activities, directions for games that can be played at home, a list of mathematics-related books to check out over vacation, and a sneak preview of what your child will be learning in *Fifth Grade Everyday Mathematics*. Enjoy your vacation!

Do-Anytime Activities

Mathematics means more when it is rooted in real-life situations. To help your child review many of the concepts he or she has learned in fourth grade, we suggest the following activities for you and your child to do together over vacation. These activities will help your child build on the skills he or she has learned this year and help prepare him or her for *Fifth Grade Everyday Mathematics*.

1 Have your child practice any multiplication and division facts that he or she has not yet mastered. Include some quick drills.

2 Provide items for your child to measure. Have your child use personal references, as well as U.S. customary and metric measuring tools.

3 Use newspapers and magazines as sources of numbers, graphs, and tables that your child may read and discuss.

4 Have your child practice multidigit multiplication and division, using the algorithms that he or she is most comfortable with.

5 Ask your child to look at advertisements and find the sale prices of items using the original prices and rates of discount; or find rates of discount using original prices and sale prices. Have your child use a calculator and calculate unit prices to determine best or better buys.

6 Continue the World Tour by reading about other countries.

Building Skills through Games

The following section lists rules for games that can be played at home. You will need a deck of number cards, which can be made from index cards or by modifying a regular deck of cards, as follows:

A regular deck of playing cards includes 54 cards (52 regular cards, plus 2 jokers). Use a permanent marker to mark some of the cards:

- Mark each of the four aces with the number 1.
- Mark each of the four queens with the number 0.
- Mark the four jacks and four kings with the numbers 11 through 18.
- Mark the two jokers with the numbers 19 and 20.

Beat the Calculator

Multiplication Facts

Materials   number cards 1–10 (4 of each); calculator

Players   3

Directions

1. One player is the "Caller," one is the "Calculator," and one is the "Brain."

2. Shuffle the deck of cards and place it facedown.

3. The Caller draws two cards from the number deck and asks for their product.

4. The Calculator solves the problem with a calculator. The Brain solves it without a calculator. The Caller decides who got the answer first.

5. The Caller continues to draw two cards at a time from the number deck and asks for their product.

6. Players trade roles every 10 turns or so.

Example The Caller draws a 10 and 7 and calls out "10 times 7." The Brain and the Calculator solve the problem.
The Caller decides who got the answer first.

10	7
01	L

Variation 1: To practice extended multiplication facts, have the Caller draw two cards from the number deck and attach a 0 to either one of the factors or to both factors, before asking for the product.

Example If the Caller turns over a 4 and a 6, he or she may make up any one of the following problems:

4	6
4	9

4 * 60   40 * 6   40 * 60

Variation 2: Use a full set of number cards: 4 each of the numbers 1–10, and 1 each of the numbers 11–20.

Family Letter, *continued*

Building Skills through Games (cont.)

Name That Number

Materials   1 complete deck of number cards

Players   2 or 3

Object of the game To collect the most cards

Directions

1. Shuffle the cards and deal five cards to each player. Place the remaining cards number-side down. Turn over the top card and place it beside the deck. This is the **target number** for the round.

2. Players try to match the target number by adding, subtracting, multiplying, or dividing the numbers on as many of their cards as possible. A card may only be used once.

3. Players write their solutions on a sheet of paper or a slate. When players have written their best solutions:

   • They set aside the cards they used to name the target number.

   • Replace them by drawing new cards from the top of the deck.

   • Put the old target number on the bottom of the deck.

   • Turn over a new target number, and play another hand.

4. Play continues until there are not enough cards left to replace all of the players' cards. The player who sets aside more cards wins the game.

Example Target number: 16   A player's cards: [7] [5] [8] [2] [10]

Some possible solutions:

10 + 8 − 2 = 16 (*three cards used*)

7 * 2 + 10 − 8 = 16 (*four cards used*)

8 / 2 + 10 + 7 − 5 = 16 (*all five cards used*)

The player sets aside the cards used to make a solution and draws the same number of cards from the top of the deck.

Vacation Reading with a Mathematical Twist

Books can contribute to children's learning by presenting mathematics in a combination of real-world and imaginary contexts. The titles listed below were recommended by teachers who use *Everyday Mathematics* in their classrooms. They are organized by mathematical topic. Visit your local library and check out these mathematics-related books with your child.

Geometry

The Boy with Square Eyes by Juliet Snape

A Cloak for the Dreamer by Aileen Friedman

The Greedy Triangle by Marilyn Burns

Measurement

The Magic School Bus Inside the Earth by Joanna Cole

Anno's Flea Market by Mitsumasa Anno

The Hundred Penny Box by Sharon Bell Mathis

Numeration

Alexander, Who Used to be Rich Last Sunday by Judith Viorst

If You Made a Million by David M. Schwartz

Fraction Action by Loreen Leedy

How Much Is a Million? by David M. Schwartz

Operations

Anno's Mysterious Multiplying Jar by Masaichiro Anno

Bunches and Bunches of Bunnies by Louise Mathews

The King's Chessboard by David Birch

One Hundred Hungry Ants by Elinor J. Pinczes

A Remainder of One by Elinor J. Pinczes

Patterns, Functions, and Sequences

Eight Hands Round by Ann Whitford Paul

Visual Magic by David Thomas

Reference Frames

The Magic School Bus: Inside the Human Body by Joanna Cole

Pigs on a Blanket by Amy Axelrod

Looking Ahead: Fifth Grade Everyday Mathematics

Next year your child will …

• Develop skills with decimals and percents

• Continue to practice multiplication and division skills, including operations with decimals

• Investigate methods for solving problems using mathematics in everyday situations

• Work with number lines, times, dates, and rates

• Collect, organize, describe, and interpret numerical data

• Further explore the properties, relationships, and measurement of 2- and 3-dimensional objects

• Read, write, and use whole numbers, fractions, decimals, percents, negative numbers, and exponential notation

• Explore scientific notation

Again, thank you for all of your support this year. Have fun continuing your child's mathematical experiences throughout the vacation!